Praise for *How to Have A Match Made in He*
A Transformational Approach to Dating, Re

"Hallelujah, a relationship book that makes sense! *F*
Heaven delivers simple yet powerful principles and g
examples of people who made huge progress in their ⌐⌐ ⌐y loving and
accepting themselves. I resonate deeply with the Kanes teachings and know with
absolute confidence that anyone who puts these ideas into practice is in for a
richer, more rewarding love life. The linked videos provide a brilliant asset, bringing the individuals and couples to life. At a time when so many people struggle
with relationships, this book can serve as a significant roadmap to connection
with self and a perfect partner."
- Alan Cohen, author of *Don't Get Lucky, Get Smart*

"The most important relationship you will ever have is the one with yourself.
The Kanes understand this, so they begin at the source working outward.
Cultivating an understanding of the effect we have on ourselves, those around us
and finally the world as a whole allows us to be an instrument for greater change.
How to Have A Match Made in Heaven, is an indispensable tool that should be
on everyone's shelf, no matter your relationship status."
- Amit Goswami, PhD, theoretical physicist, acclaimed worldwide speaker,
author of *How Quantum Activism Can Save Civilization*

"Honesty and communication are crucial to the success of any relationship and
Ariel and Shya Kane are empowering people in every part of the world to enjoy
thriving, enduring relationships by learning to be honest with themselves and
those they love and improve communication skills. The tools and mindset strategies you will gain from these pages are timeless and highly effective; to invest in
this book is to invest in your happiness for a lifetime."
- Ivan Misner, Ph.D., *NY Times* bestselling author and founder of BNI®

"From childhood, we are brainwashed by fairy tales about 'falling in love and
ng happily ever after.' With the help of Ariel and Shya Kane's book, you will
how to retain that enthusiasm for love while being able to deal with the
orld problems every relationship is bound to encounter. They help you to
nderstand yourself and your actions, thus leading to a more complete
f all the important relationships in your life."
- Betsey Chasse, film maker, co-creator of
the hit documentary *"What the BLEEP Do We Know!?"*

oking for the kind of relationship the Kanes have. Some maybe
have already found it, but for anyone who is still searching,
finding and creating a 'match made in heaven', this latest
l Shya offers tried and tested advice with real-life stories and
r confidence, clarify what you're looking for, and enhance
the right relationship for you."
anaging editor, *Watkins MIND BODY SPIRIT Magazine*

"Read *How to Have A Match Made in Heaven* and you will actually feel the joy and well being you've always wanted as you sink into its pages. With their revolutionary use of videos you will experience Ariel & Shya's compassionate wisdom and find your life transforming along with their clients!"
  - Menna van Praag, best-selling author of *Men, Money & Chocolate*

"*How to Have A Match Made in Heaven* will transform your relationships and your life. Their practical ideas, their insight and their real life stories will educate you, inspire you and help you create loving relationships. The Kanes' ground breaking use of companion videos and audios brings relationships alive in a new and exciting way."
  - David Riklan, founder & president of SelfGrowth.com,
  the leading self-improvement site on Yahoo & Google

"As always, Ariel and Shya Kane have managed to hone in on the exact triggers for what makes or breaks relationships. Their insightful advice will bring a remarkable clarity to your own situation, as well as plenty of solutions for true fulfillment."
  - Sonia von Matt Stoddard, *Awareness Magazine*

"Building a life with true partnership is possible - and it can even be fun and passionate! Ariel & Shya Kane show you how, through words and images, in this remarkable book. If a magical relationship is what you dream of, read this book and watch the accompanying videos to see what possibilities are open to you."
  - Alex Jamieson, author, chef, and health counselor

"Good information is valuable, but there's nothing like experiencing the lesson. This is where the Kanes excel. This is no sterile "How to" guide. Wonderfully illustrated through actual events and experiences of their clients and themselves, you "feel" the teachings. Feeling is what makes it real. Read *How to Have A Match Made in Heaven* and create your own heavenly relationship."
  - Neil Garvey, Publisher, *Creations Magazine*

"It was a pleasure to to read Ariel and Shya Kane's latest work, *How to Have A Match Made in Heaven*. With many years of experience working with individuals and couples, Ariel and Shya explore this fertile terrain with compassion and clarity. This book is a gift to anyone who wishes to have healthier and happier relationships."
  - Paul English, Publisher, *New York Spirit Magazine*

"The Kanes' new book will not only help readers put troubled relationships on track, but it will also help transform an already "good" relationship into "extraordinary" one."
  - Mary Arsenault, Publisher, *Wis...*

"In *How to Have A Match Made in Heaven* Ariel and Shya offer guidance on the power of really listening to another. Through helpful stories and anecdotes, the reader leaves with a new and understanding of, how to create fulfilling, loving relationship."
  - Marni Galison, President and Founder of Sunday...

Praise for *How to Create A Magical Relationship: The 3 Simple Ideas That Will Instantaneously Transform Your Love Life*

2007 Nautilus Book Award: **Winner,** category of
Relationships / Men & Women's Issues. *"...a profound journey into the world of relationships...filled with simple but powerful principles."*

2007 Eric Hoffer Award: **Notable Winner,** category of Health/Self-Help

2007 *ForeWord Magazine* Book of the Year Award:
Finalist, categories of Family & Relationships and Self-Help

"A masterpiece...unprecedented by any other relationship genre book this reviewer has ever come across."
- Awareness Magazine

"Years of therapy cannot touch what the Kanes can do in minutes... 10 stars for this outstanding work"
- Dr. Maryel McKinley

"The secrets to magical and fulfilling relationships are all here – there's no need to look further."
- Stephen Gawtry, Editor, The Watkins Review

"A fresh new approach to age old problems."
- New York Spirit Magazine

"...truly a masterpiece of the self-help genre that is destined to become the first 'line of defense' for troubled relationships."
- Mary A. Arsenault, Publisher, Wisdom Magazine

"...you need to read this most incredible book that just might change the way you look at yourself, your partner, and yes – your relationship."
- Inner Tapestry, Maine's Holistic Journal

"A well-written book with lots of positive self-affirming directions and the first of the self-help books about living in the moment that effectively tackles the problem of relationships. This is a highly recommended book."
- Harold McFarland,
Readers Preference Reviews & Midwest Book Review

"The Kanes are really on to something. The book reads easily, not dancing around serious issues, and not getting bogged down in self-help vernacular."
- New York Resident Magazine

"plenty of wisdom...plenty of gold"
- Kirkus Reviews

"Ariel and Shya Kane's book *Working on Your Relationship Doesn't Work* will help you create vital, supportive partnerships that flow smoothly day in and day out, not just when things are easy."
- *Nexus Magazine*

"...excellent...easy-to-read...a strong guide for those looking for direction in their relationships."
- *ForeWord Magazine*

Praise for *Working on Yourself Doesn't Work: The 3 Simple Ideas That Will Instantaneously Transform Your Life*

"Don't let the title mislead you. *Working on Yourself Doesn't Work* is not about the futility of self-improvement but rather about the effortlessness of transformation.... A simple, easy-to read book with a valuable message that can take you through the swamp of the mind into the clarity and brilliance of the moment."
- Kim Stevenson, *Whole Life Times Magazine*

"I strongly recommend this book. Ariel & Shya Kane are at the forefront in the field of personal transformation and have much to offer anyone who wants a more meaningful and fulfilling life."
- Paul English, Publisher, *New York Spirit Magazine*

"#1 Best Book Buy. 10+ RATING! A 'must' for the library of every seeker of truth!"
- *Awareness Magazine*

#1 Best Seller in Self-Help/Personal Transformation & Satisfaction categories.
- Amazon.com

"This warm, accessible book will illuminate and befriend your transformation."
- Mary Nurrie Stearns, Editor, *Personal Transformation Magazine*

"This book is a must read. One to have on your bookshelf and to share with your friends."
- *To Your Health Magazine*

"Ariel and Shya Kane actually 'walk the talk'.... This simple yet profound book teaches us how to live in the moment. *Working on Yourself Doesn't Work* is refreshing, truthful, sincere, and authentic and written with insightfulness and clarity."
- Dr. Maryel McKinley

"In an era of technological revolutions affecting how we work and how we communicate, the Kanes are creating a revolution in how we live."
— Andrew Gideon, Vice President, TAG Online, Inc.

"As a physicist, I don't know how they do it, but my life has been transformed by being around the Kanes. When serious life events come up – prostate cancer, my son disabled by a brain tumor, losing a job due to downsizing – I have been able to remain on-center and engaged in my life, not a victim. The Kanes' approach to living has had a dramatic impact on my happiness and effectiveness. I highly recommend their seminars and their new book which explains their transformational technique to everyone."
— William R. Ellis, PhD,
Vice President, Advanced Technology, Raytheon

Praise for *Being Here: Modern Day Tales of Enlightenment*

"This little gem of a book injects all the 'how to' directly into the reader's bloodstream, engaging the imagination.... Its deceptively simple format – stories – cracks open amazing possibilities for transformation."
— *ForeWord Magazine*

"Prescription for the good life...recommended for public libraries... inspirational."
— *Library Journal*

"Astounding.... If you're looking for enlightenment, then you need look no further than this book."
— David Riklan, Founder, SelfGrowth.com

"A must for every self-help book shelf!"
— Dr. Maryel McKinley

"This is a book of ordinary everyday moments, yet profound moments, helping us all navigate our daily experiences with the resonation of universal truths of the ages."
— *Inner Tapestry*

"An enlightened approach to the difficulties we all face in our life journey."
— *Wisdom Magazine*

"Ariel and Shya Kane have done it again in producing yet another masterpiece."
— *Love in Santa Fe Magazine*

"Sincerely helpful.... This book delivers."
— *New York Spirit Magazine*

How to Have
A Match Made in Heaven

*A Transformational Approach
to Dating, Relating and Marriage*

ARIEL & SHYA KANE

Library of Congress Cataloging-in-Publication Data

Kane, Ariel.
   How to have a match made in heaven : a
transformational approach to dating, relating and
marriage / by Ariel & Shya Kane.
   p. cm.
   Includes index.
   ISBN-13: 978-1-888043-02-0
   ISBN-10: 1-888043-02-4

   1. Interpersonal relations. 2. Dating (Social
customs) 3. Marriage. I. Kane, Shya. II. Title.

   HM1106.K36 2012   158.1
              QBI11-600231

Library of Congress Control Number: 2011945143

This book is dedicated to those individuals
who are highlighted in the videos and radio shows
throughout this book. Your honesty, courage and
willingness to be seen are inspirational, indeed.

CONTENTS

PREFACE

Virtually everyone we meet shows an interest in relating well with others. Many are in search of a mate, perhaps starting to date again after a divorce, having been widowed, or after a long hiatus from the dating scene. Others are just starting out for the first time, never having ventured into the realm of dating before. Still others are in conflicted relationships and many marriages have lost their fire. And then, some people have really good relationships or marriages but are hungry for all that is possible in a union between two people. Through it all, we have seen certain basic ideas and principles come to light. When these are recognized and mastered, you will not only have a healthy relationship, you will also move into the realm of a Match Made in Heaven.

Recently, a woman said to us, "Not everyone can have a Match Made in Heaven like you two have." That started us thinking. We realized that although she was accurate, that doesn't mean that you can't have one. In this book we will outline the keys that will support you in enjoying Heaven on Earth in relationship.

As we stated in our first book, *Working on Yourself Doesn't Work: The Three Simple Ideas That Will Instantaneously Transform Your Life:*

Heaven on Earth is happening simultaneously with
the way our lives are showing up—right now in this
moment. The trick is to be able to access this co-existing
state day in, day out, moment by moment—not just
when you are in pleasant, ideal circumstances.

Since 1987 we have acted as catalysts for thousands
of individuals and couples, guiding them toward
effective communication and personal transformation.
Our seminars are organic, interactive events, and one
of the most amazing components is the participants
themselves. During an evening event where some
people are meeting us for the first time, we find many
who are willing to speak out about their greatest
hopes, their deepest concerns and their biggest life
challenges. We are consistently humbled and awed
by the greatness of those whom we have met around
the world.

In 2009, as a natural extension to our seminars,
we started an online subscription series, *The Premium
Excellence Club*, where people signed up to receive special articles, to access a Q&A with us, and to watch video
mini-sessions of us working with individuals and couples.
This program has been an effective way for people to
get a dose of Instantaneous Transformation
delivered into their email inbox each week. As
we amassed a wide array of these videos, we were
continually moved by the generosity of those
who sat with us. In a public format, they were
willing to ask the most private and intimate of questions. It has been a true blessing to watch their faces
as they have garnered the courage to ask a question
and listen to our transformational perspective. The
camera has captured their faces, body postures and
their whole demeanor as their lives transformed in an
instant.

One day we were watching a video mini-session in which we were working with a woman named Christiane. A few minutes in we suddenly realized that her situation was such a perfect example of how people get stuck in relating. It was too brilliant not to share with more people. Christiane seemed to come to life as we identified some of the archetypical "mistakes" that people make in relationships and how these life choices can send them down an unsatisfying road for the rest of their lives. It was just too good to keep only for ourselves and those who were currently members of our subscription series. It was time to get permission to share Christiane's journey with the world, as well as the stories of many others who have inspired us. Today we are delighted that so many courageous people have allowed and encouraged us to share their true stories with you.

We clearly owe a debt of gratitude to our clients who have been so giving of their time and so honest about their abilities to relate. Join us as they so generously expose their private thoughts and foibles so that others can discover How to Have A Match Made in Heaven right along with them. We invite you to step into these very special moments as each person reveals a facet of the gem of a heavenly relationship.

In our award-winning book, *How to Create a Magical Relationship: The Three Simple Ideas That Will Instantaneously Transform Your Love Life*, we changed the names of people whose stories we used as examples. In this ground-breaking book, however, not only are we leaving the majority of people's names intact, but we are also offering online access to the videos themselves.

Please note that we have taken literary license when incorporating the videos into the text of *How to Have A Match Made in Heaven*. We decided that a simple

transcript of our conversations with these folks might
fall short in recreating their brilliance as they literally
"pop" off the screen. It is our intention to have these
people and their life stories come alive for you. We
hope we have done them justice.

1

PUT YOUR LISTENING
EARS ON

*I*t doesn't matter where you are in the cycle of dating, relating or marriage, one of the most important skill sets to develop and hone is that of listening—*really* listening—to hear what your partner (or anyone else) is saying from his or her point of view. In fact our definition of True Listening is to listen to hear what another is saying from his or her perspective. This sounds pretty simple, and you may think that you do this already. But do you really?

Our minds are complex and brilliant micropro-cessors, capable of performing many tasks in an infinitely small time frame. That's one of the reasons why slowing yourself down to simply listen is often a challenge. Think about this: If someone says some-thing you like, don't you automatically agree with it in your mind?

Let's take a look at the process of agreeing and disagreeing for a moment. In order to agree, there is a step that comes first: comparing what is being said with what you already know. If what someone is saying is consistent with your current knowledge base and beliefs, then you agree. If it doesn't, then you disagree. But all of this takes place in a nanosecond. Ask yourself the following questions:

1. Do you sometimes catch yourself rushing ahead in your thoughts as you finish someone else's sentence?
2. Do you ever lose the sense of what another has to say because you're busy holding onto what you want to say when your turn arrives?
3. Do you automatically agree and disagree while conversing with another?

If the answer to any of the above questions is "Yes," don't worry. You are normal. In fact, having a mind that works this way is part of being human. What we are suggesting here is purposefully slowing down and listening to hear what another is saying from his or her perspective. Not to see if you know it already. Not to see if it adversely affects an agenda of yours. And not to agree or disagree, but simply to hear it from the other's perspective.

Here are some hints on how to supercharge your listening skill set. Begin by listening with your eyes as well as your ears. Look directly at your partner or the person you are dating or spending the evening with.

Engage as if you are listening to the words and the essence of what is being said, not only through your ears but through your eyes as well.

If you are listening to someone on the phone, be aware that your eyes are still processing information. If you're reading emails, watching a muted television show, or working on other things with your eyes, you'll miss the nuances of what is being said. You are perfectly capable of toggling back and forth between both activities but you will not do either well. And you will not be building a sense of intimacy. You will simply hear what you expect to hear—not what is actually being said.

2

INTIMACY BEGINS
WITH YOU

$\mathcal{U}$rsula, a rosy-cheeked, cherubic Swiss woman in her mid-40s with short brown hair, sat down and had a conversation with us one Monday afternoon. It was the day after she had attended our weekend workshop in Hamburg, Germany and she was one of several people who came to participate in recording some video mini-sessions with us. Over the course of that seminar we spoke with participants about being in the moment, about really being here for one's life rather than trying to get ahead or focusing on getting somewhere. We encouraged people to truly listen to one another.

It's so easy to get fixated on ourselves as we apply what's being said to our lives. It's easy to tune out when the conversation doesn't meet our preferences or address our interests. For instance, someone may attend one of our seminars with the primary goal of learning how to find a mate or "fix" their relationship. As a result, this person will most likely drift away in his or her thoughts rather than listening closely when the topic turns to sports or child rearing.

Ursula had spent the weekend with us, purposefully turning her attention to whatever was happening in that moment. It had a profound impact on her experience of herself and of the people and things in her life. As a result, she immediately had a direct experience of living her life in an intimate manner rather than talking to herself about what she would prefer.

Ursula had been a client and friend of ours for several years, and as we sat down with her to record it was obvious to us that something new had happened, something special had taken place that weekend. On that chilly fall day in a cozy apartment her eyes misted up and her voice was filled with emotion. All of those who came to participate in our video sessions were riveted.

"Life is so exciting," Ursula said. "I attended a weekend workshop with you here in Hamburg and I think I discovered for the first time what intimacy means."

She paused briefly as she collected herself. Close to tears, she took a breath and continued. "Today I went shopping with a few girlfriends and the world was full of intimate moments, everywhere, with everybody—even the salesperson."

She strove to articulate just how special her day had been. It was a challenge for her to put into words her experience of the sweetness and magnificence of simply being alive. Suddenly, for no apparent reason, she had felt free to be herself and her day had unfolded with a childlike sense of wonder.

"My day had a lightness about it," she said. "I was just living my life, not thinking about it, not thinking about how to go about it. I didn't make the decision, 'I'll sing along with Abba' in the store. It just happened. I spontaneously sang along with the tune that came on over the store's sound system. When I noticed some trousers or saw a piece of jewelry, I easily walked over and looked at it. I felt intimate with *things* as well as with people."

Ursula was obviously inspired, as she continued to speak about the details of her day. It hadn't occurred to her before that intimacy was an experience that happens when you are being in the moment rather than something that happens with only special people, under special circumstances. She had had meaningful exchanges with her friends and with the waitress who served her salad. The actual events of her day had been rather ordinary but her experience had transformed.

"I have a question about these intimate moments," Ariel said. "Did any of them include men?"

Ursula paused. She looked into space as she scanned her memory of the day. The room was silent. Several seconds passed.

"Not that I remember," she said softly. But in the next moment, her face suddenly came alight. "Yes, yes! There were some with men!" she exclaimed, laughing delightedly.

"Good," Ariel said. "It's really beautiful that you can feel intimate with your pants and your salad and your girlfriends. I'm not making fun of that. It's just that it sounds kind of funny."

"It *is* funny," Ursula said.

"But I would start including men," Ariel said, glancing at Shya. "Because the world is populated with them."

"At least half the world," Shya said.

"And they're quite wonderful, you know," Ariel added.

"Yes, I can see that," Ursula replied, while looking at Shya. Her eyes welled up as she became emotional once again. "I can see *you*," she said.

"Oh, that's nice. I appreciate that," Shya replied.

"It is," she said. "And it's fun, too!"

"Uh-hum," he said and we sat for a moment enjoying each other's company.

"It's just so moving to discover more and more in my life," Ursula said, earnestly. "This feeling of intimacy includes more and more people."

"That's good," Shya said.

"And *men*," she added.

"That's kind of like saying 'Amen,'" Ariel joked.

"Yes. Amen!" Ursula said.

It was a sweet and intimate moment, shared by the three of us and by all who were watching us in the room. "I can't thank you enough," Ursula said. "I've been coming to these courses for some time now, I think about seven or eight years, and I'm always surprised that there's more. There's more depth and there's more width and more fun and more of me and more to experience with anybody I meet. I like that very much. Thank you!"

We were happy for Ursula. She truly caught the essence of a transformational approach to living one's life, which extends to a Transformational Approach to Dating, Relating and Marriage. She was no longer treating herself as broken or deficient in any way. She wasn't lost in trying to get ahead, find a boyfriend, improve her life or fix those around her. She wasn't distracted by complaints or hanging onto the story of her past and her plans for the future. Ursula had discovered that intimacy began with herself. She was awash in the experience of "Being Here," and her life was heavenly indeed.

Intimacy Begins with You
TransformationMadeEasy.com/matchmadeinheaven

HOW TO ACCESS THE VIDEOS
AND RADIO SHOWS

If you would like to watch the companion videos and access the radio shows that form the basis for *How to Have A Match Made in Heaven*, simply go to:

www.TransformationMadeEasy.com/matchmadeinheaven

and follow the instructions on that page. You may want to bookmark it in your browser to make it easy to access in the future.

You can also access the videos and radio shows using the above quick response (QR) code with a smartphone.

3

BE A SCIENTIST

$\mathscr{A}$lthough dating, relating and marriage are very personal, the best way to approach relationship is by de-personalizing things. Our approach is anthropological. An anthropologist studies cultures, interested in how that culture is put together, not in judging how it functions. In order to have a Match Made in Heaven through a Transformational Approach to Dating, Relating and Marriage, awareness is key.

AWARENESS: AN ANTHROPOLOGICAL/ TRANSFORMATIONAL POINT OF VIEW

Awareness is the noncritical, nonjudgmental witnessing or seeing of anything. It allows for what is seen without adding the element of "doing" something to alter it. When using awareness, hold in abeyance your ideas of good and bad, right and wrong, and better and worse so you can simply observe something without assigning value for or against it. When you hold these ideas in abeyance, you retain your values—you don't lose anything. You are simply setting your judgments aside to view more clearly your behaviors or ways of interacting with yourself, your environment and others.

Why not develop an anthropological perspective similar to ours? As we mentioned, an anthropologist observes cultures nonjudgmentally, without a comparison to any standard. He or she watches in order to observe the way that culture functions. People do not normally bring this non-self-critical, nonjudgmental observation to their way of relating. We invite you to be a scientist, exploring a culture of one—yourself and the way you relate.

If you are looking to *change* the way you relate, it will be an arduous task, filled with judgments and self-recriminations. When you are working to change, you look for those aspects of your behavior or your partner's behavior that you deem as wrong, inappropriate or inadequate. Then you set out on a course of correcting the things that you have identified as the problem.

But let's talk about this for a moment. The things that you see as problematic were ingrained in you by the culture in which you were raised. Your ideas of right/wrong, good/bad, beautiful/ugly are based in the cultural standards that you absorbed in early childhood. You were trained to look for what was wrong and then to do something to fix it. This is the paradigm of change, not transformation.

With transformation, simply seeing is enough to facilitate resolution.

It's about looking to see the "is-ness" of something rather than judging how you or your partner behaves. Again, it is about observing behaviors rather than picking apart and finding fault with the way you relate.

The idea that simply seeing something can resolve your problems may sound odd, impossible or somehow incomplete. Don't worry. In the pages ahead we will demonstrate possibilities that you have not yet considered. We understand that you have ways of relating that you would like to change, address or get rid of. But what we are suggesting is a far easier and more effective way to go about resolving your "problems" than picking on yourself and/or your partner.

There is the possibility of Instantaneous Transformation.

THE THREE PRINCIPLES OF INSTANTANEOUS TRANSFORMATION

Although we delve deeply into the Three Principles of Instantaneous Transformation in both *Working on Yourself Doesn't Work* and in *How to Create a Magical Relationship*, we feel it is important to outline them here as well. This is because they form a support structure for moving your relationship from mundane to magical and they are the backbone of a Match Made in Heaven. If you are not yet familiar with our principles, don't worry. Although we lay out the basic ideas here, there are many examples throughout this book that will move the concepts into reality so the principles come alive for you.

The First Principle of Instantaneous Transformation:
What you Resist Persists and Grows Stronger
(and dominates your life and your relationships).

You may be familiar with a law of physics that states: For every action there is an equal and opposite reaction. This law is also the basis for the First Principle of Instantaneous Transformation. We once had a conversation with a physicist who put this in simple layman's terms. He said to us, "When you push on something, it pushes back with an equal amount of force." When you apply this idea to relationship you can see how things get stuck.

For instance, have you ever noticed something about your partner you didn't like or tried to change? But the more you worked to change him or her, the more he or she persisted in staying the same? Do you ever feel like you are nagging him or her either out loud or in your thoughts? When this is the case, your disagreements with your partner eventually dominate your life and your relationship until they are your primary focus. You no longer see the good points, those things that attracted you to your partner in the first place. You see only faults—or what you consider to be his or her faults. So once again, the First Principle is that anything you resist will persist, it will continue, and it will, in fact, dominate your relationship.

The Second Principle of Instantaneous Transformation:
No two things can occupy the same space
at the same time.

To make this principle easier to grasp, think in terms of a moment in time. A snap of your fingers will do. If you were to snap your fingers right now, in the instant your fingers snapped, where were you? Were you seated in a chair? If so, then you could only have been sitting where you were in that moment in time. In other words, you can only be exactly where you are and how you are in each instant.

To illustrate this point a bit further, have you ever paused a television show, a DVD or a video? Did the actor on the screen get stuck with a goofy look on his face? The action was stopped in an instant and he could only be caught with his mouth open or with his eyes at half-mast.

We all have preferences and ideas that dictate how we should be in any given moment of our lives. In our fantasies we each should be in a harmonious, nurturing,

blessed relationship and all the relationships that we have
with those around us should move smoothly. We should
feel well in ourselves, confident and satisfied. But what if
you don't? What if you just had a fight with your spouse?
What if you can't find anyone to date?

This is the time to take an anthropological approach.
The state of your relationship or your ability to relate is
simply a snapshot in time. In this moment you can only
be exactly the way you are and where you are. This is
not a good thing or a bad thing because good and bad
are part of the paradigm of change, as opposed to the
paradigm of transformation. It simply is. Life shows up
in a series of moments of now, and in *this* moment of
now you can only be exactly the way you are. That is the
Second Principle.

**The Third Principle of Instantaneous Transformation:
Anything that you allow to be exactly as it is will
complete itself and dissolve all on its own.**

If you let things actually be the way they are, without
trying to change or fix them, without judging them as
good or bad or right or wrong, they will complete themselves and disappear.

This principle is often the hardest to grasp because we have
been trained to think that simply seeing something is not
enough for it to complete itself. We think we should feel bad
for our transgressions and we resolve to do better in the future. We think we should look at a problem, find a solution
and then work to implement the new strategy for success.

But let's look at your life honestly for a moment. Hasn't
everything that you've tried to get rid of stuck around on
some level? Those things that you push against, when
you've said, "I've got to change, I shouldn't be like that,"
don't resolve.

Awareness, a nonjudgmental investigation, can free you from old patterns, even things that have gone on for years that you've resisted, tried to get rid of and made New Year's resolutions about. If you allow yourself to simply be with anything, it loses its power over you. But if you resist an old pattern of behavior, you give it power.

When you see something without judging or resisting it, in the instant that you see it, it is resolved. This may be hard for our minds to grasp because it is so outside our normal reality, in which we have been trained to *do* something with what we see. But noticing your way of relating is enough to facilitate resolution in an instant.

THE THREE PRINCIPLES AND YOUR CLEVER MIND

Now that you have the basics for the Three Principles of Instantaneous Transformation, notice how clever your mind is as it tries to rearrange things so you can still "change" for the better. In other words, you are likely to turn the principles into a system for change in order to "see" something and "be" with it so it will complete itself and disappear. This is the First Principle in disguise. It takes practice to observe how you are being and relating without adding a judgment to it, without adding the agenda to be a better you or to try and fix your partner.

Change is Linear – This Book Isn't

In a perfect, linear world, one thing follows the next in a logical sequence that progresses toward a logical, desired conclusion. In this fantasy world, you date, relate and then happily marry. But life isn't like that.

Originally, we thought about breaking down this book into those logical steps. We thought about starting with dating, moving on to relating and then, of course, the final destination would be marriage. But the act of relating is much more organic than that. It has twists of fate and is influenced by many factors. As you will discover in the pages ahead, a Match Made in Heaven is not an achievement, but rather a lifestyle. As such, it requires that you focus your attention on how you relate and that you continue to romance your partner. You will find chapters that address dating, for instance, sprinkled throughout the entire book.

Whether you are currently dating, in a relationship or already married, see if you can relax around your agenda to get ahead and improve your ability to relate by investing in this moment of now. As you get practiced at being here, your way of relating will naturally expand all on its own. There is no need to make resolutions to be a better you. There is no need to make mental notes on how to behave.

Just put your listening ears on. By simply "listening" (reading to hear what we have to say from our perspective) without doing anything with what is said, our approach will naturally integrate into your way of being.

But we want to warn you. This will be a challenge because you are intelligent and have been trained that if you see something that is "flawed" or wrong, you should try to do something about it in order to change it. You have been enculturated into thinking that making resolutions will help you in the future. You have had the idea instilled in you that someday your life will be better than it is right now. It is highly likely that you have not been trained to fully invest in this moment as if it were the pinnacle of your life—which it is.

Don't worry. No need to change. Transformation is already happening. It happens in an instant and you reap the benefits over time. This is one of the paradoxes of a transformational approach. Your ability to relate transforms in an instant and yet with consistency, the effects are also cumulative.

By the way, your ability to transform happens in an instant but your mind never catches up. It is a machine that is filled with tapes based on themes that have been put together over a lifetime that repeatedly play back to you. If you just notice your thoughts without holding them as the truth, they will lose their power over your life and over your ability to relate.

4

A MATCH MADE IN HEAVEN
STARTS WITH YOU

We are what we think.
All that we are arises with our thoughts.
With our thoughts we make the world.
                              - Buddha

In order to build a strong foundation for relationship, you must first investigate your relationship with yourself. If you are unkind to yourself, you will ultimately be unkind to anyone who forms a partnership with you. When you connect with another, he or she becomes an extension of you. Ultimately, you will pick on that person in the same manner that you pick on yourself. At first, you may only be critical of him or her in your thoughts. But soon, thoughts translate into attitudes, and attitudes dictate actions. Think back to disagreements you've had with others in your life. Haven't the worst fights or meanest arguments happened with those you love?

If after reading this book, you only had one benefit—being kind to yourself—we would consider it an overwhelming success.

That is because Heaven on Earth
begin with you. If you are in turmoil inside,
there will be no peace in your relationship.

In order to let go of repetitive, negative thoughts about yourself, it's always a good idea to become aware of your inner commentary without judging what you discover. As you bring awareness to all that you say to yourself about yourself in the privacy of your thoughts, you will notice that your thoughts aren't static. In other words, in certain types of situations, your thoughts will mechanically take a negative bent and during other situations, they won't. If you start with the supposition that your thoughts are always negative or self-deprecating, then you won't notice the nuances of your inner life and you won't register the times when you are already being kind to yourself.

In the next section, we invite you to listen in on a conversation we had with our friend and client, Stefanie, in a garden one sunny, breezy morning. It was a lovely spring day, the Monday following one of our weekend seminars.

KINDNESS BEGINS WITH YOU

Stefanie is a beautiful middle-aged woman with lustrous wavy white and grey hair that settles gently on her shoulders. As we began, she was quick to lay out what she thought was her problem. "I realize that I hold grudges against people," she said with a slightly distasteful look on her face.

Holding grudges seemed to leave a bad taste in her mouth.

"I find it hard to forgive other people," she went on, "if they've been unkind to me or if they've done something that I don't like."

"Well, it starts with you," Ariel said.

For a moment, Stefanie looked a little thrown by Ariel's comment. She seemed surprised. Perhaps she expected us to judge her for holding grudges as much as she judged herself. This wasn't the tack she expected either of us to take.

"I'd be willing to bet that you have a hard time forgiving yourself if you do the littlest thing that you think is either not nice or inappropriate," suggested Shya. "You judge yourself if you do something that you think isn't good enough, or if you make a 'mistake.'"

Stefanie laughed in recognition as the sun fell on her hair, lighting it up like a halo. "Oh yes," she admitted, "I'm very harsh with myself, even if I stumble on a stairway."

HOW YOU TREAT YOURSELF IS HOW YOU TREAT ANOTHER

As Stefanie mentioned stumbling, it triggered a memory of the first time we met her, a number of years ago, at one of our Hamburg workshops. In the building where we rented space, the entrances to the rooms were elevated by a few inches and Shya stumbled on one of them. Witnessing this, Stefanie had blurted out, "You can't be *that* enlightened. You tripped!"

"Oh God," Stefanie exclaimed, simultaneously laughing and wincing as she recalled the incident, too. Her comment still embarrassed her all of these years later.

"Stefanie, don't feel badly about it," said Ariel. "That isn't an example of you being unkind or harsh to Shya. It's really an example of how you talk to yourself."

"Yes," Shya continued, "in that moment, you simply treated me the way you treat yourself."

"That's true," Stefanie said, her face softening. "I would have said that to myself, at least in my mind."

"No," Ariel said, "you would have been much harsher if you were talking to yourself."

"Yes," Stefanie agreed, "I would have called myself an idiot or something worse."

"Okay," Shya said, "just notice all the times you call yourself an 'idiot' and don't make yourself wrong for it. Simply notice the mechanical nature of picking on yourself and see if you can notice it without making yourself wrong, because you can't help but pick on yourself when you do. If you see it and don't judge it as good or bad or right or wrong, that's enough for it to complete itself in an instant," he said, snapping his fingers. "It doesn't take time. It happens in an instant. And then you get better at it. By the way, this is the Third Principle of Instantaneous Transformation."

Stefanie had been listening to him with rapt attention, her mouth slightly open. "That's wonderful," she said, clearly delighted by the possibility, "because I often catch myself being harsh with myself and then I say, 'You shouldn't be so harsh with yourself!'" She was laughing now.

"But you see," Shya said with a grin, "that's the First Principle. If you disagree with something, it will stick around. Anything you resist, sticks around. So if you say 'shouldn't,' that will keep it from disappearing."

"You can either treat that harshness as a problem," Ariel explained, "and say 'Oh, I shouldn't do that!' or you can start recognizing when you're harsh. Simply observe it or notice it. Then your inner commentary might shift to something like, 'Huh, I'm upset. I didn't catch something. Something happened that disturbed me and I didn't see it.' Because there are times when you'll do the exact same thing but will have a completely different reaction to it. One time you'll laugh and say, 'Oops, I just tripped,' but in another instance you'll call yourself an idiot.

"When you're being tough with yourself, chances are you're already upset. Maybe there was something you forgot to say to somebody at work or perhaps you let something happen that didn't feel right to you. Looking at how you talk to yourself can be an exciting adventure of possibilities, as opposed to one more thing to be hard on yourself about."

"That's wonderful," Stefanie said softly. "It just gives me a feeling of relief and peace, because I'm not doing it wrong."

"You can't do it wrong!" we exclaimed in unison.

"You can only do it exactly as you're doing it in the current moment of your life," Shya said.

Ariel suddenly sang, "And that's Transformation."

"Thank you so much," Stephanie said. Her face looked alive, the wind swept through her hair, and the feeling of relief and peace that she'd spoken of was visible in the softness of her face and the delight in her eyes. It was as though her whole body had let go of every harsh word she'd ever spoken or thought. Stefanie was suddenly feeling the true sweetness of her heart and the softness of life all around her. It happened in an instant. And that's Transformation!

Kindness Begins with You
TransformationMadeEasy.com/matchmadeinheaven

DON'T JUDGE YOURSELF
FOR JUDGING YOURSELF

Have you ever noticed how harsh you are with yourself? You'd probably be shocked if someone recorded all your thoughts and then played them back to you. You are so used to the way you speak to yourself, you may not realize the harsh tone you take. When this is the case, you won't really notice when you speak to your partner in the same way.

In order to be kinder to yourself and others, you first have to pay attention to the way you currently behave. It starts by noticing when you're harsh and when you use derogatory terms or an abrasive tone. When you notice this behavior and don't judge yourself for doing it, then the behavior will dwindle away on its own (Third Principle). If, however, you criticize yourself for what you see, then you're resisting your behavior. That will only mean that despite your best intentions, you won't be able to stop. You'll be trapped in a cycle of behaving "badly," then feeling "badly" and then behaving "badly" all over again. This is the First Principle of Instantaneous Transformation:

When you are harsh with yourself for being harsh, it simply reinforces the behavior. In other words, what you resist persists, grows stronger, and dominates your life.

If you have been unkind to your partner, seeing this behavior without judging what you see is enough to dissolve it. But it's still a really good idea to apologize. A Transformational Approach to Dating, Relating and Marriage is paradoxical: On one hand, there's nothing to be done with what you see. You don't need to judge yourself, since judging yourself leads to more of the behavior. You don't need to make a resolution to do better in the future, either. Yet, if you have been unkind, saying "I'm sorry!" and meaning it can mend a world of hurts.

NOTICING WHEN YOU'RE ALREADY UPSET

You may think that certain circumstances are inherently upsetting or frustrating, that they make you upset and cause you to respond in an abrasive manner. But if you take a look, you'll notice that when you react strongly to something, oftentimes you were already upset.

Your experience of driving in heavy traffic is a good example. If you're feeling calm and at peace with the world, someone can cut in front of you and it barely makes a ripple in your day. You are likely to mentally shrug it off and allow the other vehicle to go in front of you. But on another day, when you're already out of sorts and someone cuts into your lane, your reaction is likely to be far different because you're already upset. The challenge is that most of us have been taught to blame the circumstances for our upsets rather than seeing ourselves as primed to react.

DON'T BLAME THE TRIGGER

Upsets can range from a low-level grumble to an explosion. Let's look at the explosive nature of a bullet as an analogy for an upset. A bullet is a projectile in a casing that is backed by combustible material, gunpowder and a primer. When the trigger is pulled, the gun's firing pin hits the bullet and a chemical reaction ignites the primer, which ignites the gunpowder, which causes a rapid expansion of gases. This expansion forces the projectile out through the barrel. If you had a bullet in a casing minus the gunpowder or the primer, when you pulled the trigger, there would be no reaction. The gun is loaded only when the bullet has a charge.

In the same way, it's easy to blame your partner or a circumstance or even yourself for doing something "wrong" when in fact you are simply pre-charged. For example, if you've had a "bad day" at work or if you've had a frustrating day with your kids, when you get together with your spouse, it's far easier to snap at him or her as if your partner is the cause of your upset.

**Blaming something outside of yourself
perpetuates recurring upsets.**

If you simply bring awareness to how it is that you function, without judging yourself for what you see, or blaming something or someone for causing them, these recurring upsets will lose their hold over you and with practice, you will be free of them.

STICKS AND STONES

Have you ever heard the saying, "Sticks and stones will break my bones but words will never hurt me?" It's not true. Words can bruise a relationship. And like a piece of fruit, with enough bruising, it goes rotten. Now is a good time to look at how you fight and when doing so, take a nonjudgmental approach.

How have you been enculturated to disagree with your environment and those with whom you relate? Do you curse? Do you yell? Do you say hateful things and throw objects around? Do you hit things or people? Or do you get quiet and withdrawn? Do you blame people or circumstances for how you feel, as though they were responsible for your feelings? Perhaps you feel depressed, drink to excess and mope around. Or maybe you "turn a cold shoulder" and sleep facing the wall. Still another way to fight is to stay out late with your friends over and over again, regardless of your spouse's wishes. Or you promise to be home at a certain time and you come home much later. Or perhaps you are habitually late wherever you go.

Most people shy away from looking at how they fight. Fighting is often viewed as "bad" or something to be

ashamed of, to sweep under the rug or to gather agreement about from your friends. If you want to have a
Match Made in Heaven, an anthropological approach
will support you in this. It is important to look and see
how you behave when you're upset. It is far easier to dissolve those habitual ways of fighting if you honestly see
them and don't judge what you see. And don't forget,
if you said something that is hurtful, employing those
three golden words, *I am sorry,* and meaning them, can
oftentimes make things right again.

5

THE STORY OF YOUR LIFE

*H*ave you ever stopped to think how much the story you tell yourself about your life defines you? How old were you when you put together the notion of who you are? When did you form your ideas about relationships and your ability to relate? The story of your life contains ideas about who you are that are very well rehearsed. These ideas have been refined by the telling and retelling of them, first to yourself in your thoughts, and then to your family, friends and anyone else who will listen.

Most people find that the idea of letting go of who they are to discover their potential is a frightening prospect. You may not like your life or how you relate, but it is *you*. Your story, however, contains many erroneous and limiting impressions as recorded from a childish point of view that severely limit what is possible today. This tall tale was put together partially from the culture/family that you were born into. It includes those things that that culture/family believed to be true. Early childhood experiences, based in that original way of looking at life, i.e., the cultural backdrop, all contribute to the story of who you consider yourself to be. Your limitations are part of that fable. What you thought you were good at or not good at became an extension of that story. Then you gathered evidence to prove your point of view. This is especially true of your perceived faults or limitations. You have used social situations and interactions to prove that your beliefs about yourself are true. These beliefs actually precede you into each moment of your life and dictate how you will act in each moment, based on the past. It can be equated to looking in the rearview mirror while driving to determine which way to turn next, and then wondering why your car has so many dings.

The mind is a survival machine. It gathers and stores incidents that were potentially threatening, as if those events that you survived and your behavior during those moments actually *caused* your survival. Have you considered the idea that you survived *in spite of* your foibles or ways of relating? The mind constantly gathers evidence to prove itself right, but that evidence-gathering is biased in the following way:

The mind looks through its data to find out why you survived. But the mind's sampling is limited to what it already knows or holds to be true. These ideas are the only possibilities from the mind's point of view for your survival. It follows that serendipitous events outside the mind's current paradigm or system of seeing do not exist in the logic system of this mind. As a result, the conclusions your mind reaches are flawed by the limited sampling of possibility through which it reaches its conclusions. And yet this limited basis of who you know yourself to be has perpetuated the story of your life and who you think you are.

This story may not be to your liking. It may say you need to work on yourself or fix certain aspects of your life or upbringing in order to be a better you. But this story is the known. Stepping outside the known is frightening and may appear to be threatening to your survival.

For sure, it is threatening to the story's survival because the story gives you an identity. But that identity gives you a false sense of security and a false sense of control over your life.

For instance, on the morning news program *The Today Show*, there is a weatherman, Al Roker, who is famous for having lost more than 100 pounds and 20 suit sizes. Mr. Roker was obese and it was his dying father's wish that he would lose the excess weight. We recall an interview the newsman did after he had undergone gastric bypass surgery and the change in his physicality was highlighted. He said that one of the biggest challenges was not the surgery or the dietary changes but rather his concern that people would no longer like him if he were not "the funny, fat weatherman." Although Mr. Roker's extreme weight was dangerous enough to be life threatening, he was reluctant to let it go because his mind had identified his body mass as integral to his success and survival.

YOUR MIND IS LIKE A PANINI MACHINE

A Panini machine is really an upscale grilled cheese sandwich maker. If you take two pieces of bread, some mozzarella cheese, a slice of tomato, some fresh basil, and place it in a Panini machine, it will be mixed together into a gooey, toasted meal. Once the cheese has melted, it is virtually impossible to fully separate all the ingredients of the sandwich. They have been combined into a single entity. That's just like soup. Once it's made, you can no longer remove a single ingredient.

In much the same way, your mind is a recording device which sandwiches all the ingredients of an event together and forms a strategy for going forward. If you've been exposed to one style of relating as a child, you are likely to unwittingly search for this type of "love" as an adult. But what if your relationship "sandwich" includes the idea that you are unattractive or not datable? How would that story affect your life today? Let's take a look at how such an idea affected the life of a friend of ours.

A WHOLE NEW WORLD

In a quiet living room we sat down with our friend, Annina. It was a lovely spring morning and there were approximately a dozen of us ready to video a series of mini-sessions. These courageous individuals had volunteered to ask their very private questions in a public format.

We have come to realize that there is a commonality in people where their humanity speaks across genders, nationalities, ages and religious differences. Very diverse groups of individuals can see themselves in one another when they stop and take a look. It is always generous of people when they are willing not only to ask a question so they can get something for themselves, but when they're also willing to give to others at the same time.

At first glance, Annina is a rather stocky woman in her mid-40s, but if you slow down a bit and really look at her, you are likely to find her round face and short brown hair rather pixyish. With her soft-spoken ways and easy blush, you would no doubt see that Annina is like a delicate flower.

In a very earnest manner, Annina told us of a recent happening in her life. "After I came back from the workshop with you both in Costa Rica," she said, "I got a new passport. The other one had broken. I hadn't noticed it until the immigration officer at Newark Airport told me, 'Madam, you need a new passport.' The photo page was plastic and it had started ripping."

We weren't sure where Annina was taking us but she looked so intent, it was easy to keep listening as she continued. "This is the sixth passport that I've had in my life and for the first time, I was happy with the picture."

She said this with a shy smile.

We felt warm inside that Annina was finally able to see her beauty. And this was just the beginning. Little did we know that there was much more to come as she continued. "When I got the old passport back with the hole punched in it, I put it with the other four outdated ones. And when I was doing this, I had a look at all of my previous passports. I just looked at the pictures and to my surprise, I loved every one of them! I thought to myself, 'Well, she looks so attractive. She looked so attractive when she was 16, then when she was 28...' and so it was so marvelous."

We also found her realizations marvelous. Annina's story about her lack of attractiveness had colored her perception of herself for at least 30 years. Her story had acted as a set of blinders blotting out the beauty that was so evident to us when we were in her presence.

"When you were 16, did you think you were attractive?" Ariel asked.

"No, not at all. I hated the picture."

"Did you think that you were attractive at 28?"

"No," she said emphatically. "No, I didn't. This was the first time that I was really happy with a picture of myself and I thought it was attractive. I look attractive."

This moment was too good to let slide by. What a wonderful discovery Annina had just made. How lovely to finally see past an old story to realize that you are really, truly attractive. For fun, we asked her to say it again. She was confused, as hesitantly she said, "It's the first time...I look attractive."

It was worth repeating once again, so we asked, "Could you say that one more time?"

Softly, sweetly, she replied, "I look attractive now. And it's a good feeling."

Ariel said, "You were attractive all along, but you

couldn't see it because your internal conversation said something different."

Looking as if yet another door had just opened, Annina replied, "It must have been this way. Yes."

At this point, Annina was not only standing on the threshold of a long-closed room, she was preparing to step into a whole new world. With a wistful expression she said, "I wonder in what other context of my life I haven't been allowing myself to see my own attractiveness."

"Well, I have a context for you," Shya said gently. "You haven't looked at me yet in this conversation."

His observation was quiet, yet the truth of it was thunderous. Annina turned to face him directly. She did not pause to think about the statement. She didn't stop to get defensive. She simply looked without judging what she saw and said, "That's true." And then looking further, as if she were answering an age-old mystery, she repeated, "Yes, that is true."

"So here's another possibility of what you may be missing, Annina. They're called 'men.'" Shya spoke in his straightforward style. "You might be attractive to men."

"Yes, yes," she said, laughing. "That might be a little dangerous!"

"It might be," Shya said, "but it might be fun."

With a sense of wonder in her voice, she replied, "Yes, it might be fun as well."

While Annina and Shya chuckled companionably, Ariel said, "Almost half the planet is populated by men, Annina."

It was an intimate moment among the three of us and it was also being shared by the video team and those who were in attendance.

"What happens when you look at him?" Ariel asked, directing Annina's attention back to Shya.

Annina blushed prettily and laughed, "I'm in the same way surprised as I was when I saw my picture of the new passport."

"And what is that?" Shya asked. "What are you surprised by?"

"That I didn't see it before."

"See what before?"

"See how good it feels. And the whole new world that comes with looking at you."

"Yes," Shya replied.

Annina sat quietly in her seat, looking as if she were awakening from a dream. "And with looking at you comes the possibility of the other half of the world—the world of men."

It was a sweet moment. Annina looked at Shya and he at her. There was a simplicity and grace. Annina's smile was beatific.

"From the moment you looked at him, Annina, you've become even more beautiful," Ariel said.

"Yes, I even realized it myself, that I'm..." Annina's smile grew wider as she searched for words to express herself. "I think I'm using another pair of muscles to smile which I don't normally use! It's lovely."

"Yes, you are," Shya said, "You are very lovely."

"Thank you!" she said. "So much has happened to me since knowing you both." Her shoulders were relaxed. Annina was resting comfortably in herself.

"You've been thinking that you know who you are rather than discovering who you are," Shya said. "Now is a good time to discover who you are."

"Yes," she replied, "this idea of discovering myself came up during your weekend workshop, too. I realized that if I risk not knowing who I am until the moment arrives, then I don't need to have a notion of myself in advance."

We nodded. She had discovered something very important. Oftentimes people think they need to know what to say or who to be in advance in order to be okay, in order to give themselves an identity so they can feel secure or comfortable.

"I don't find this scary anymore," Annina said. "It's thrilling and makes life a lot of fun!"

"You look very lovely, Annina," Shya said.

She blushed once more, "Thank you. Thank you. Thank you so much."

We all sat for a moment as everyone in the room took a collective breath. We turned the cameras off and the recording of the mini-session was over. Others began shifting in their seats, preparing for their turn to talk with us, but Annina wasn't done yet. She rose to her feet and crossed the space between herself and where Shya was seated. It was in actuality a short distance but Annina was crossing a great divide. Leaning over, she wrapped her arms around his neck and buried her face in his shoulder. Her muffled voice said once again, "Thank you. Thank you so much."

They hugged a little longer as we all enjoyed the moment. It was as if she had finally thrown open the door to her heart to include men in her life. It was a sacred moment, a beautiful thing to behold. And Annina was really, truly attractive. It was a whole new world.

A Whole New World
TransformationMadeEasy.com/matchmadeinheaven

YOUR LIFE STORY DEFINES YOU

Let's pause here to look at the story of your life. It contains your life history as recorded by you. It also includes things told to you by others and it's colored by your cultural background. People don't simply experience their lives; rather, they have been taught how to interpret events. For instance, a young child may learn that he or she is "bad" or "dirty" when a parent catches him or her playing with their private parts. It was obvious that Annina had developed a common type of story about her attractiveness. Many a youngster has come up with this erroneous idea. What about you?

We are not suggesting that you get rid of your life story.
We are encouraging you to become aware of your
internal script without judging yourself for its content
and without necessarily believing it.

BEYOND THE STORY

It has been said that for a chick to hatch, a world must first be destroyed. The egg must be cracked open for the chick to be born. This is also true about our ideas of who we are. If we believe what we've told ourselves about our lives, we will never look further to see what else is possible. The story itself will dictate how our life circumstances are interpreted. It keeps repeating and finding evidence to prove itself right about who you are and what you are capable of. Therefore, in order to discover your true self, you have to step outside the story that you inherited from your childhood. You can do this if you get into the current moment of your life directly through your experience, not based on your past.

For most of us this is a very challenging prospect. Although we may not like the story of our lives, it is in fact all we know ourselves to be. When looking at your life, try borrowing the idea from Annina that if you're willing to risk not knowing who you are until the moment arrives, you won't need a notion of yourself in advance. In this way you can discover who you are rather than have the past repeat itself.

GETTING PAST YOUR PAST

It was a brisk fall day when Candice sat down with us. We had assembled in our living room in New Jersey with a group of folks who had come to record another series of mini-sessions with us. We didn't actually know Candice very well. She was a friend of our assistant, Val, and as we began, she appeared hesitant to speak.

The fire crackled merrily behind us as this lovely young woman began her exploration into how to improve her ability to relate. It was clear from her demeanor that a Match Made in Heaven wasn't yet even a remote possibility for her because she was locked in the past, trying in vain to sort out her childhood. She had been taught that in order to move forward, you have to fix your past.

"I've been struggling for a while. I think I'm stuck in the past with a lot of stuff that happened and it's hard for me to get over that," she began.

"What about your past are you struggling with?" we asked.

"The fact that my parents got a divorce when I was 13 or 14 years old. My mom is the one who left. Most of the time, you don't really see the mothers leaving the household. But she just left with her boyfriend and my whole family completely imploded. We were a tight-knit family and when she left and we found out what was going on, that was destroyed. So that stuck with me and I'm stuck there."

It was obvious that Candice was in a bind. The story

itself was compelling, as if the circumstances of her adolescence had locked her in a room from which there was
no escape. We were sure she was surprised by the key that
Shya handed her.

"Now look, Candice," he said lightly. "This is a great
'bad' story. It has all the earmarks of good drama. They
could use it as a script for 'All My Children,' or some
other soap opera."

A smile flitted across Candice's face as Shya continued.
"You could be like a normal person and have this be the
pivotal point of what's determining your life going forward in time. Or you can let go of your story about your
mother, your story about your father, your story about
your family imploding. You've said that before. Imploding was too good a word for you not to have used it
before."

"Yes, it was," Candice agreed.

"This is a familiar story that you've told yourself and
other people ever since you were 13," Shya said.

At first Candice didn't see that she had rehearsed her
story, but as we bantered back and forth in a light-hearted manner, she relaxed. She saw that she had crystallized
that story while talking about it during therapy. What
she had presented to us that morning was a distillation
of the woeful tale she had repeated to herself throughout
the long years of her youth.

People think their story is who they are, but Candice
was much, much more than a story about her mother
leaving. We pointed out that the fact that her mother
left did not have to determine how she related to her
husband or the quality of her life.

Ariel said, "Many people think they can't have a good
relationship, Candice, because they've never seen one or
because they came from a broken family. But your life
is unique. It can't be compared to other people, and it

didn't happen wrongly. It's not like you're starting with a handicap.

"Our approach is not psychotherapeutic. It's anthropological in that you simply notice what has happened in order to see it without judging it. Anything that you resist from your past dominates your life. Obviously, something that was as monumental to a young girl as her parents dissolving their marriage is something anyone would resist.

"It sounds like it happened in a rather inelegant way," Ariel continued. "You were so surprised that your mother left with her boyfriend, it caused a break that was a huge life change. And you weren't alone in the situation. You had a whole familial unit that resisted it.

"But you're at a new place now. There is a whole new possibility where you don't use your parents' breakup as the reference point for how you relate. It's about being here in each moment and relating to whoever is sitting across from you."

"You see," Shya added, "you've considered yourself special and broken because you came from a divorced family."

From the look on her face, it was obvious that Candice didn't agree. But the truth of Shya's statement and the ramifications of living from this part of her story were about to be borne out.

"I think that I do go back to my parent's breakup in my thoughts," Candice conceded. "When I try to move forward and do something, I say to myself, 'I can't do that because my mom left,' and I feel like I'm worthless. I feel like I can't continue accomplishing things that I would like to accomplish. And I do reference her in my mind. But now I'm at the point that I want to just let that be. I want to walk away from it and detach. Even though I know it happened, I want to leave it back where it happened. I don't want it to be here with me now."

"Okay," Ariel said, "let's go back to the First Principle of Instantaneous Transformation for a moment. If you don't want your mother's leaving to be here with you now, you're resisting it. And anything you resist persists and dominates your life. If you resist the fact that she left, you are going to keep her departure around as an active component in how you relate. Anything you allow to be, lets you be. That's the Third Principle."

"Let's take a look at the reality of divorce for a moment," Shya said. "More than 50% of marriages in the United States end in divorce. So if your parents' relationship ended in divorce, you're normal, not special."

Candice looked a bit reluctant to let go. Her mother's sudden departure was such a huge component in the story of who she was, it had become the go-to excuse for why she couldn't move forward in her life. But the way Candice was looking at things is very common. Each of us has tucked away some "bad" stories that we can pull out as a reason for our lack of success. As we looked around the room at the people in attendance, it was easy to see the reasons they had given themselves for not moving forward in their lives and in their relationships. There were days when each of them felt worthless and their stories came to the foreground:

- I can't because I'm too old.
- I can't because I'm too young.
- I can't because my last relationship was a disaster.
- I can't because I'm too fat.
- I can't because my parents fought.
- I can't because I don't have the right education. And on and on.

"The story itself doesn't matter," Ariel said. "It's just where you go when you need a story as a reason not to go forward. It's not about getting rid of that story. It's about not accessing it as an excuse to do or not do things."

Shya took over from there. "If you leave your story alone and look at what you want in your life in this moment without referencing back to determine whether you can or can't do something, suddenly you're in control of your own life. Suddenly, that story loses all power over your life.

"In fact, the Second Principle of Instantaneous Transformation says you can only be exactly where you are in this moment of now. You can't be any different. You have to be sitting right here, right now across from us, Candice, because you are. In this moment of now, you can't be any different. But if you think about your early life right now, you're not here, you're back there. Then you lose the opportunity of having this magical moment called 'your life' right now and now and now.

"Candice, you're an extraordinary woman, including your mother's leaving—not in spite of it, not because of it. But it happened and trying to get rid of it lops off a part of you. It's like this floor here. Part of what makes it beautiful is the grain of the wood. All that happened in your childhood is part of the grain of the wood called 'Candice.' If you get rid of the bits you don't like, you no longer have a strong foundation. It becomes holey and porous and it doesn't work. If you grind down all the grain, there will be none of you left."

"Yes," she said. "That's something I struggle with. I keep going back and forth in my mind thinking that I could be better. I keep saying to myself that I could do this better and I could do that better."

"But that's not true," Shya said. Raising his right hand, he added, "Be different than you are right now."

He snapped his fingers. "Oops, too late. So how could you have been better than you were? Be better than you are right *now*," he said again with a snap of the fingers. "Too late. That moment went by. It's right now. Ready? Let's try again."

As Shya prepared to snap his fingers to signify a moment in time, Candice began to smile.

"Don't be smiling right *now*. Nope. You had to have been smiling because…"

"I couldn't help it." Candice supplied.

"That's right. In this moment, you can only be how you are. That means you can only be exactly as you are in every moment of your life, including what went before. If it didn't happen the way it did, you couldn't be here right now. So I personally thank your mother for leaving because otherwise we may never have met you. I would be sitting here talking to an empty chair. That would be rather embarrassing, don't you think?" Shya asked.

Nodding thoughtfully, Candice said, "It does make sense, but I think it's going to take time. Definitely."

"It does and it doesn't take time," Ariel explained. "That's one of the paradoxes of transformation. It's instantaneous and it's also cumulative. Setting down your story happens in an instant. The more often you let go of using your mother's departure as a touchstone or as the reason for anything, the easier it'll become. With practice you'll get better at leaving it alone, but you've been trained to think that this should be a long and hard process. You think it's going to be difficult and that you have to overcome obstacles. But what if it isn't difficult?"

"If you set down your story about all your obstacles and difficulties in life," Shya continued, "you no longer have it. That's one of the beauties of our Costa Rican Adventure. People come to the group, they spend six days where they're not living their story every day and they don't have the things around them that reinforce it. Suddenly they forget they even had one, and they discover their greatness. It's also the beauty of our weekends because you get so involved in what's happening with other people, you forget your own story. If you forget it long enough, you don't know who you are. Then you can discover who you are without referencing an old idea of yourself but rather by looking and seeing."

"You don't have to trust me—but trust me," Ariel said as Candice laughed. "You are magnificent."

Shya punctuated the moment with, "Really."

Looking thoughtful, as if she had a whole new set of options, Candice smiled once again and said, "Thank you."

"Yes," Shya replied, "Thank *you!*"

 Getting Past Your Past
TransformationMadeEasy.com/matchmadeinheaven

6

JUST RELAX

*I*t is very likely that you are currently reading this book with the desire to "get somewhere," to get ahead, to improve the quality of your relationship or at the very least, to discover how to effectively date. Of course this is understandable. Why would you read a book on the theme of relationships if you didn't have an interest in improving the way you relate? However, we suggest relaxing around your wish to expand.

In the next section we're going to meet John, a very intelligent, highly educated man who was struggling with dating. In John's case, his intelligence and drive to succeed were actually getting in his way.

When you relax into the moment, expansion happens on its own.

As you read his story, see if you can relax around your aspirations. You just might find it key to your current relationship challenges.

YOU HAVE ARRIVED

As we sat with John in our living room that morning, his desire to date and confusion about how to go about it were palpable. John, a man in his late 40s with a mustache and hint of grey in his sideburns, was wearing a

grey button-down dress shirt. His opening statement revealed his way of thinking and his conundrum. It was
easy to see that he judged himself for his lack of dates.

"I want to step into my greatness, my potential, and
I feel like I'm not doing that at some level," he said. "I
have my doctorate, I have books coming out, I think I'm
datable and it seems like maybe I'm more comfortable
being sort of a languishing victim."

John's ideas about himself were clearly heartfelt, but as
he put them forth you could see the tension these theories created in him. It bled into his voice, his shoulders
crept up and his jaw was tense.

Much to John's relief, Ariel leaned forward and
engaged, "You have a theory about what you need to
do and you're putting pressure on yourself to do that in
order to be a better you." Waving her hands in front of
her as if they were wands that could wipe away his tension, she said, "If I had to give you advice, I'd say, relax."

It was as if John's body language shouted, "Relax?
What do you mean, relax?" This was a foreign concept
to him. He was used to making a plan and following an
agenda to get ahead. He was accustomed to using his
vast intellect to identify problems and solve them. Surely
relaxing wasn't the answer.

Ariel was undaunted. "Relax, John, relax," she repeated. "You're over-thinking it. Just relax." It was obvious
that saying these words was not going to do the trick.
It's far easier to think about relaxing than actually do it.
Especially if you believe that relaxing is not the answer.

Taking a different tack, Ariel said, "Shya and I were
out on the river with a master teacher named Andrew
who was teaching us Spey casting, a style of casting with
a two-handed fly rod. I was talking to him about my
technique when he said, 'You know, this is probably what
you talk about in your relationship courses: Don't over-

think it. Just relax.' I'm passing on Andrew's advice to you. Don't over-think it—just relax. If anything, John, when I've seen you in a social situation, you put this pressure on yourself to step into your brilliance, as you said, or your potential. This isn't producing the intimacy you want or the dates you desire. But if you relax when you're near people, they'll come to you, they'll be invited to converse with you."

"Your intelligence is getting in the way," Shya continued. "You have all these theories about how you need to be more appropriate or eligible to date. You're not allowing yourself just to be the man that you are with people. You put pressure on yourself to do it within the framework of what you know and you're guided by what you have decided was cool. These ideas were probably formed in your early teens."

"Women like men who are approachable," Ariel said.

"Hmm," he replied. John's face had been awash with a wide array of thoughts. His countenance flitted from curious to impatient, from annoyed to interested.

"Women like approachable," Ariel repeated. "You don't have to keep coming so far forward. You don't have to try so hard."

"Have fun," Shya suggested.

"Okay," John reluctantly replied.

"Listen rather than trying to talk. Because, you know, listening is really an amazing thing. When you pay attention to someone else, they get interested in you because what most people want is attention. And you see, they want attention so badly they talk at other people to get attention, but it usually turns others off. Try listening."

"Okay."

"Get interested in others, John," Shya said.

"Okay," John replied again.

"Can you feel how even now you're a little bit mentally

on the edge of your chair trying to hear the tips, trying to get somewhere?"

A light bulb seemed to turn on. John was becoming aware of his forward thinking momentum.

"There's no rest in you, John. It would be okay to relax—really."

John took a breath. That was the beginning of space between the moments.

"Slow down," Shya said with compassion.

"Really, John," said Ariel, "you've arrived. You're this great man, but you've had this pressure to produce and get somewhere. You've got your doctorate, you have books coming out, it's great. But even in the videos that you produced for your website, there was this pressure to be upbeat." Ariel took a moment, took a breath and released it. "It's as if you've run your race and now you can relax."

With a slight shift of his head, it was as if John said, "Really?" Our words were barely computing. They didn't fit with what he knew. John just didn't know what was "wrong" that caused the disconnect in his ability to date and relate but surely it couldn't be as simple as relaxing.

"You put together a schematic when you were a child," Shya said. "It included the structure of the right way to be a man and what you had to accomplish in your life. Now you've accomplished most of it, John, but you haven't looked at the structure you put in place that keeps pushing you to accomplish *more*. There's no resting in you because you constantly think you haven't accomplished enough."

Unconvinced, John slowly nodded, "Uh-hum."

"I'll give you the key," Ariel said.

"Please give him the key," Shya added.

"It's really important," Ariel continued, suppressing a grin. "You have to slow down enough to let a woman catch you."

"And they will, if you give them the chance," Shya said with the voice of experience. John made another non-committal sound of agreement but his shoulders dropped and his body relaxed. He graced us with a lovely smile.

"Trust me on that one," Ariel said.

"Okay, I do," John said softly. "Thank you guys."

"You're really welcome," we replied.

John's thanks had been heartfelt. It was warm and full of meaning. Our reply was just as heartfelt. He had slowed down. A connection had been made. You could see the great man that had been hidden behind his intellect and the tension to get ahead. It was as if the air itself had softened. John had arrived into the moment and it was sweet and rich and instantaneously he was handsome and accessible and dateable. This man was approachable. It was a lovely moment and we all savored the flavor of being here. Now let's move on to Holly and see how John took his next step.

 Just Relax
TransformationMadeEasy.com/matchmadeinheaven

JOHN'S HIDDEN DATE

Holly, an attractive woman in her late 40s with auburn hair and a curvaceous graceful figure asked John to come to her home to help her move some furniture that was too heavy for her. At an ensuing Monday evening seminar in Manhattan, she stood up to talk about how sweet he'd been to give her a hand and what a fun time they'd had together. Holly had had plenty of unsatisfying dates with men who did not return her interest or who quickly showed that they were not compatible. As she was talking, John was beaming from his seat and it became quickly apparent that they'd missed a fundamental truth. Because they were "just friends," they'd missed the fact that the afternoon they'd spent together was a date. It had been so easy and effortless and natural that the truth of the situation had passed them by unnoticed.

"That was a date!" Ariel said.

"Wow. You're right!" Holly replied. "I didn't realize it."

Holly looked at John, he looked at her, and they saw each other in a new light.

Not long after, Holly and John had another "casual" get together but somewhere during that encounter she asked if he would spend the night. We heard that he enthusiastically said, "Yes!" It was so sweet to see them together after that—often leaning toward one another when sitting in one of our seminars. They had the relaxed ease of two people who had been together far longer than they actually had been. Soon John let go of his apartment and moved in with her.

We realized that it was true. John relaxed and a woman caught him.

HOW ABOUT YOU?

Now is the time for you to relax as well. If you're dating or contemplating dating again, you may be reading this section with the desire to glean tips that will help you with that process. If you've been married for years, you may be skimming through this section to get on to the information that applies to you. You may erroneously think that you're "beyond the dating stage" and may be rushing forward to find the marriage parts. But dating itself is a key building block for any relationship or marriage. In fact, when a couple gets into trouble, they have often forgotten to woo each other. They have forgotten how to date. It's easy to forget when there are bills to be paid and children to be fed or when you're busy trying to make your relationship "go somewhere."

The two of us are on a succession of dates. They have already lasted 30 years and we expect a lifetime of them. Sometimes we stop what we're doing when one or the other of us will say, "Want to take a date with me out to the mailbox?" Then we slip on our shoes and go out our front door. The screen door makes a creaking salute, and we often hold hands as we head out into our driveway, our feet crunching on the gravel. It's a time to feel the air and smell the greenery and see the sun slanting through the trees. Or perhaps it's a time to slide over the snow and watch the bare branches clatter in the wind. But it's always a time just for us. Getting the mail is an excuse to be together.

Of course we don't actually need an excuse since we live and work together, but we make one anyway. We have dates while doing the dishes and others while making a trip to the grocery store. We have a library date when we go together to pick out books on CD to listen to during the hour-long ride to New York City where we work. And occasionally over the years, we've even had a date in the emergency room as one or the other of us needed medical attention. It's all an intimate adventure if you're there for it.

SUSAN'S FIRST DATE

It was still cool at 6:30 in the morning as we strolled barefoot with Susan down Costa Rica's Manuel Antonio beach. We were in the midst of one of our Costa Rican Self Discovery Adventures that we hold each winter. People come from all over the world to join us and use it as a time to get away from the normal routine of their lives and relax. It's an opportunity to look at the mechanics of their lives in a gentle, lush environment without judging what they discover, a time to play and let their lives unfold.

On this particular morning, Susan was talking with us about her relationships—or more accurately put, her lack of them. We've known Susan for years and she is such a great lady. Perhaps you know someone just like her. She's a mover and a shaker at work, well respected in her field, someone whom people admire. In her early 40s, she's pretty, slim, personable, smart, humble, and absolutely adores baseball. In short, she's a dream gal for most any man.

And yet, over the years we've known her, Susan has not had much luck with relationships. Traditionally, she falls head over heels for a guy and after several months or occasionally a year or two, the relationship ends. Gradually Susan stopped telling people when she really liked someone. It became embarrassing for her to admit when "things didn't work out" and yet another relationship was over.

We asked her what was happening with dating. Grimacing, she replied, "I'm taking a break. I just don't see the point. I never have trouble attracting guys—it just never lasts. Something must be wrong with me."

Discarding the idea that there was something "wrong" with her, we looked at her approach to dating. We encouraged her to take a transformational, anthropological approach—like a scientist observing a culture of one, herself—by looking non-judgmentally, with awareness. When you do this, the best place to start is where you are. Exactly where you are—in this moment.

"How are you approaching things *right now?*" we asked her. "Start to bring awareness to this moment, this instant, not someday."

As we looked at her life in that moment, it became obvious that in her attempt to fix her "problem" and set things in order and make for a better future, Susan missed so much—the caress of the breeze as it tousled her hair, the sand between her toes, the steady lap of the surf.

As we conversed, it became apparent that Susan was rarely present to where she was. She was habitually driving forward for some desired result that was supposed to make her happy or fulfilled or better—in the future. It became apparent even in how she approached the conversation. For Susan it was a challenge simply to walk with us. She was so accomplished at thinking and strategizing that she kept losing sight of where she was. She missed the lovely shells, the sea foam and the way her muscles moved as she walked. She either charged ahead or got lost in thought and barely moved at all.

We asked her if she had ever dated more than one person at a time. She looked surprised by the question, as if we were suggesting that she was somehow "loose" or unwholesome. So we explained, "Do you ever meet one fellow for lunch on Tuesday and another for a movie on Friday night," asked Ariel, "so that you can see who might really work for you before you jump ahead into a relationship?"

Sheepishly, she said, "No."

That was when we realized that Susan had never actually "dated." Instead, she automatically married. As soon as she went out with someone, she was trying to make him "the one." Somewhere in the back of her mind he was already her mate—the perfect relationship. So she never actually dated, she went from mini-marriage to mini-marriage and this strategy kept backfiring.

We encouraged Susan to keep relaxing into herself and into her body for the next few days and forget about getting ahead. Let go of her plans to date or to not date. Just be there and have fun.

Two days later during the course, Susan piped up with excitement about her first boogie boarding experience. As she spoke, we looked around and Ralf was beaming. Ralf is an actor who is gay and married. He is accomplished at riding waves and Susan had asked him to teach her.

"I asked Ralf to teach me to boogie board," she said, "because it looked like so much fun and it was obvious that he was really good at it. At lunch we went to the beach and waded out into the water. Although I was nervous, he made it okay. I hugged the board and the next thing I knew, the wave was coming. As I stood there, I realized that this was the one—the one where I could finally learn to boogie board. Much sooner than I expected, Ralf said, 'Jump!' and I did. I made it all the way into shore! It was great."

Ralf grinned, "Susan really listened! She timed it perfectly and caught the wave."

Both Susan and Ralf were so happy. He felt smart, listened to and empowered and so did she. That was when the realization hit us. This was Susan's first date. It was the first time she had ever "gone out" with a man without the mental computer casting forward to possible futures. She was simply being there and enjoying the moment.

If Susan could bring that type of engagement to going on actual dates, where simply having fun was an experience that was complete in and of itself, not leading anywhere other than this moment, her life would transform. All it would take is awareness. She habitually planned for the future, but with awareness, Susan could now suspend her old habits and be there.

> **Having fun is a pretty powerful way
> to start any serious relationship.**

THE ART OF FLIRTING

Many times your dating life may falter or your married life may stagnate when you forget the art of flirting. If you want to reawaken your abilities, flirting is a great way to start. When we say flirting, we're not necessarily talking about making sexual advances or suggestive moves. We're talking about taking the attention off your agendas, away from your story about yourself, and engaging with the people around you. It's about being sincerely interested in the guy or gal who serves you your coffee or striking up a conversation with the person next to you in the checkout line. You can even "flirt" with inanimate objects. In other words, if you're making a meal and slamming the pan around in agitation, that's no kind of date. But if you're there for the sensuousness of a tomato or the smell of an orange, it can be a very lovely moment.

There's a difference between flirting with someone as a manipulation to get better service, such as saying "nice shirt" to the server at Starbuck's in hopes of getting more whipped cream on your drink, and actually saying "nice shirt" because you mean it.

We did a radio show dedicated to the art of flirting and a teacher named Andrea called in from Switzerland to ask a question about dating. But rather than focusing on her "problem," we asked about her teaching.

"If you're being light and playful," Ariel said, "or if you're serious and directed, in which way do your students learn better?"

"When I'm not directed. When we're just having fun," she replied.

"Well, that's what we're talking about. We're talking about flirting with your life, having fun."

"That's cool," Andrea said, "because it sounds so light."

"It is light," Shya replied. "You can flirt anywhere and everywhere. You know, people think there are only certain circumstances where they can flirt. One of the places traditionally you 'can't flirt' or have to be cautious is when you're going through security at the airport. But recently, we had a meaningful exchange with a security agent about fishing for Atlantic salmon. After seeing our gear going through the X-ray machine, one of the guards initiated a conversation with us about fishing. He wanted to know where to go, what kind of fishing flies to use, and the size of our fishing rods. As we spoke, he came alive about his own life in a light and playful way."

"Wow. That's very neat," Andrea replied, impressed with the idea as she momentarily forgot about her quest for a better date.

Ariel said, "This interaction happened because we weren't treating him as the enemy or like a piece of furniture between us and getting to our destination. He is a human being, but every day he deals with so many people who don't see him because they're going somewhere. In order to really be appropriate when you're flirting with somebody, you have to be there for it. You can't just phone it in. We're sure that the security guard also comes across a lot of people who are being nice to him so he won't hassle them. This type of manipulation never works. We were just being ourselves. When you're being yourself, Andrea, you're very attractive."

We talked more with Andrea about flirting in the traditional sense of the word, and Ariel took the lead:

"I was really good at flirting when I was on the dating scene, but the challenge was that my flirting was directed. I would look around, pick somebody who fit my picture of Mr. Right, and those were the men I actively flirted with. Eventually, I got so tired of trying to make it work out, I decided I'd just flirt with Shya because I didn't have to worry about it going somewhere. He was too old for me, in my opinion, so nothing would ever come of it. It was just a chance to go out and have some fun—no strings attached. I just really shamelessly flirted with him and he flirted back, and we started dating and we've never stopped. It's been one non-stop date. When you direct it, you miss people."

"When you only look for a certain type of person to date," Shya added, "have you recognized how you can have the same boyfriend in different bodies? How you'll pick the same type of guy over and over again?"

"Yes, I have," she said.

"Do you ever wonder why that is?"

"Yes," Andrea replied.

"In the first five or six years of a child's life," said Shya, "you imprint your whole life going forward in time until you discover awareness about your own behaviors. And so your first love was your father," Shya stated with certainty.

"Yes, yes he was."

"Your father may have been a great guy, but his mental and emotional makeup may not be a fit for you as a mate. Still, you pick people who resemble your father from the child's point of view at the age you were when you decided that daddy was your love."

"Yes, that's the truth!" Andrea said brightly. "Perfect."

"So, Andrea, that isn't the woman choosing a man to relate to. It's your conditioning as a child that determines who you choose to date. That's very dissatisfying for most people. What we're talking about is flirting indiscriminately, where you allow yourself to be playful and be there to see whoever is in front of you."

As we continued to chat with Andrea, she came alive at the prospect of flirting in general with her students, and romantically flirting with people who were outside of her normal picks for datable men. We discussed the idea of letting herself be fully herself rather than only showing what she thought was a better version of Andrea. We explained that if she only showed the parts of her that she considered acceptable to a prospective mate, she would never really relax and would start the relationship on a shaky foundation. If you're hiding pieces of yourself, you'll perpetually mistrust any relationship as it's forming. You become prey to the idea of, "He only likes me because he doesn't know me. If he knew the real me, he wouldn't be interested."

Andrea began flirting in earnest after this conversation. She began doing it everywhere—with her voice students, with her audiences when she performed and with available men, too. She's quite good at it and it's fun to see her express her beauty in such an easy and open manner. It didn't take much. She was already "flirting" some of the time. She just hadn't realized that she could approach her whole life in a flirtatious manner. It's a transformational approach to dating, relating, marriage…and life.

The Art of Flirting
TransformationMadeEasy.com/matchmadeinheaven

7

INTIMACY AND
THE PERFECT YOU

*I*t doesn't matter where you are on your journey to having a Match Made in Heaven. There is always the next opportunity to discover intimacy as well as to recognize the barriers to intimacy that crop up along the way. Being intimate is never a static thing. In any given moment, you are either moving toward closeness with another or farther away. Behind it all is your relationship with yourself.

Early on in this book, in the section entitled *Kindness Begins With You*, you may recall a conversation we had with Stefanie about being kind to herself. In that chapter we also introduced the idea that how you treat yourself, you will treat another. We discussed with Stefanie the concept of nonjudgmental seeing in relation to her tendency to be unkind or "harsh" with herself.

As you move through the barriers around being truly intimate with another, you may have a tendency to have repetitive, self-deprecating thoughts. As we explore the subject of intimacy in depth, it's worth revisiting the importance of exercising your ability to observe your foibles without finding fault with what you see.

We all have ideas about what intimacy is. We've heard about it. We've sought it out. But what is it? When most of us think of intimacy, we think of it as a euphemism for sex, something to be achieved or gotten over with. People want to have sex, but when they have it, they often want it to be over already. They are driving toward an orgasm or shrinking from the encounter, literally and figuratively closing their eyes to the entirety of the experience.

True intimacy has to do with being comfortable in your own skin. It is a willingness to engage in the current moment of your life as if it is perfect. It includes embracing your current life circumstances as if they are your choice or idea. Intimacy is being willing to be with whatever is happening in the current moment of your life.

When you're being intimate in your life, like the smell of a flower, it's not directed to only those you aim your "perfume" toward. You aren't only intimate in certain situations with a few trusted individuals. The experience of intimacy radiates and is pervasive in all aspects of your life.

Let's take a look at what may cause you to feel uncomfortable in your skin. Perhaps you have self doubts, where you look to your past to see how you have failed and then you worry that you might fail that way again or not be successful, or not be able to perform, or not look good to yourself or others. Perhaps there is the fear of being rejected. But for most people the discomfort is not so cerebral. It's a form of upset. When the mechanism of upset gets stimulated, people's fears about the future based on past embarrassing or uncomfortable moments take over. They leave the current moment of their lives and are plunged into fear about how the future is going to turn out.

There are body sensations and thought patterns associated with being upset and if you indulge them, you lose the current moment. When you were born, you didn't have an idea about what a perfect body would look like. You weren't self-conscious. You didn't have an internal conversation at all, much less about cellulite, maintaining an erection or "will I have an orgasm?" All of that came later.

Initially, you urinated and defecated when the urge arose and there was no awareness of smell or cleanliness or mess. You cried when your diapers became uncomfortable and someone changed you. As you began to grow, you were ruled by what felt good and your parent or caregiver would find you with a hand on your vagina or fondling your penis, depending on your gender.

Along with the socialization that followed came ideas about your body. You could blame how you feel towards your body on your parents but this blame would be misplaced. In truth, you absorbed their body language and values as they were training you in how to use the toilet and how to be in public without lifting your dress or rubbing up against surfaces that felt good. Your parents have absorbed the reality of their parents, who absorbed the reality of their parents, and so on back through time.

It's a challenge for most people to be with another, or even themselves, without engaging their programmed ideas about what is attractive or unattractive and what is "dirty." Let's investigate further your ideas about a "perfect" version of you and where those ideas came from.

THE PERFECT YOU

A young man emphatically stated to us, "I'll date when I lose weight!" We also know a married woman with three children who is reluctant to leave her home because she says, "I'm too fat. I don't want people to see me this way."

Where did you learn what is beautiful? Where did you learn what is ugly? Where did you learn what a perfect body looks like? How old were you when you came to these conclusions?

We were walking down the street in Paris several years ago to find ourselves taken by a body image considered to be "beautiful." We were looking at the street lamps in front of the Paris Opera House. Built in the mid-1800s, those lamps are supported by statues of naked women. These castings done in the Neo-Baroque style are curvy with rounded bellies and by today's standards they all need to go to Weight Watchers, visit Jenny Craig or at the very least, tighten their abs with a good dose of Pilates.

Our idea of a beautiful body was given to us by the culture in which we grew up. By the time we reached puberty we each had decided how we needed to look in order to have the perfect body. But by that time, we knew we never would.

One year the two of us led six weeks of consecutive courses at a conference center on Maui. The course room had an entire wall of mirrors, so we became comfortable seeing ourselves daily in shorts and even from time to time in our bikini and swimsuit. When we completed the groups, however, and rented a hotel room at the beach for a bit of R&R, we were surprised to discover that our bodies appeared sadly lacking. We realized that we were no longer living in the cloistered environment in our courses, where people were encouraged to let go of their judgmental nature. We were now looking in the same mirror where thousands of tourists before us had stood while being self-critical and we were surrounded by people in everyday life with their everyday criticisms and complaints about their bodies.

It was a lesson we never forgot. The culture that surrounds you can make a direct and immediate impact on your self-perceptions. If you want to know about your body image, begin by paying attention to your internal conversation without taking it personally.

"What?" you might say, "How can I possibly not take how I look and feel personally?"

It's easy, once you realize that your thoughts about yourself and how you look are a collection of recordings stored in your internal jukebox or MP3 player. When the circumstances apply a little pressure, they play a familiar tune.

The key to creating something new rather than playing an oldie-but-not-so-goody is awareness. The art of awareness or self-observation without self-reproach is a skill set that can be learned. It's like exercising a muscle. The more you simply see things without judging them, the better you get at neutrally observing yourself. As you discover how to be kind to yourself rather than berate yourself for the body you have, it sets you up to find motivation for living a healthy lifestyle. If every time you step on a scale or go to the gym, you find reinforcement that you're "fat," sooner or later you're going to want to quit on yourself. If every time you feel like having sex with your husband or wife you are worried about them seeing your body, it will be difficult to have the physical intimacy you crave.

Do you want to know a great secret for dissolving a negative body image? Practice your anthropological approach. Pretend you're a scientist observing a culture of one—yourself. The trick is not to judge what you see, but to neutrally observe how you function, including your thought processes. Awareness and kindness are key. If you have some extra pounds, be kind to yourself right now, not when you lose the weight and not when you continue the exercise routine that you promised yourself you would.

In this moment, you are a perfect you. If you gain or lose some weight, then you will still be you. But if you're kind to yourself right now and just notice how you are without beating up on yourself for what you see, then regardless of your weight, shape or size, you'll feel satisfied. This also applies to your sexual experience or lack of experience. If you are kind to yourself about what you don't yet know or haven't yet experienced, it is far easier to learn.

Most people are afraid that if they aren't hard on themselves, there will be no motivation to improve, no reason to move, and they will turn into the world's largest couch potato. Not true. When you are feeling satisfied and good in your own skin, there is no need to turn to comfort food. That extra cookie doesn't feel like a reward when living your life is its own reward. Don't you feel more like moving out into the world and being active in your life when you aren't being hard on yourself? When you don't pick on yourself, your actions will support a healthy lifestyle and your body is sure to follow.

8

THE PERFECT "THEM"

As you look for a mate (or look at your mate), you may want to become interested in your ideas about the perfect him or her. Chances are you've seen movies where the hero and heroine rip off their clothing in a heated frenzy and have mad passionate sex on the floor, stairs or against the wall, in all their buff and toned glory. But movies are obviously not reality. Even Julia Roberts had a body double in her famous movie, *Pretty Woman*.

Perhaps you have read magazines that tout the top 10 attributes for the best lover. On the cover, a model's body has been airbrushed until it is a perfect image of "sexy" rather than a reflection of reality.

Do you ever compare yourself or your mate to those models in magazines? We have a friend who used to work in the entertainment industry who told us that many of those "perfect" bodies are actually Franken-people: a torso from here and a head from there, legs and hips from yet a third person…stretch it a little longer…delete any wrinkles, bags, freckles or blemishes and voilà: The Perfect Him or Her.

SOMETIMES BRIGHT AND SHINY ISN'T THE BEST: A BERRY PICKER'S GUIDE TO DATING

The following story demonstrates a different approach to finding The Perfect Him or Her, as told by Ariel:

I started picking berries for money at the age of 6. My aunt Joyce took me with her to the berry fields to "help out" at her summer job and after a full day of picking strawberries (many of which made their way into my mouth), I was proud to bring home three shiny dimes for my labors. Before dinner, my mother put them in a place of honor and I went to bed that night dreaming of all the penny candy I could buy at the little store in town.

All the local kids I knew picked berries during the summer to make spending money and some worked to pay for clothes and school supplies for the year ahead. There were many growers around, so we worked the seasons: first, strawberries, then raspberries, a short crop of boysenberries (by far the easiest to pick), marionberries or blackcaps, then blackberries. In fact, picking berries was so common where I grew up, it never occurred to me until after I moved to New York at age 19 that not everyone spent summers in the berry fields.

Each summer, my mom would make us wonderful desserts featuring local fruit and at the end of the season, one of my favorites was blackberry cobbler. My sisters and I would take large metal bowls and fill them with the wild blackberries that grew by the roadside or down at the edge of the field on our property and Mom would turn them into something delightful.

Shya and I went to visit my parents for their 60th wedding anniversary one August (Congrats to Mom and Dad!), so we were there during the height of blackberry season. In order to keep fit, given all of my mother's excellent meals, Shya and I decided to take a walk on the Springwater Corridor, a 40-mile loop that was created for walking or bike riding, following an old trolley right of way. This paved walking trail has large cane blackberry bushes that grow in abundance on either side. During our walk, I picked a few berries for Shya and myself and they tasted heavenly. I actually went to bed that night dreaming of taking a large metal bowl and filling it once again for my mom.

A couple days later we went for another walk and we saw that after additional time in the sun, there were even more of these ripened dark beauties hanging in clusters, both high and low. My aunt Larrita had just brought my folks a whole crate of them so I was relieved of the need to do any serious picking and could simply focus on finding the ripest, juiciest, yummiest ones to savor— staining our tongues a dark purple.

As I was picking with Shya, I realized that his lack of experience had him reaching for those berries that I would never pick. He automatically was drawn to the bright and shiny berries glowing in the sun. They looked perfect. They looked just like the ones you would find in the store: tasty but tart—usually very tart. And so I began to teach him from an old country girl perspective how to spot and pick "black gold."

First you had to search for those berries that appeared somewhat dull—they were easy to overlook when the bright and shiny ones were hanging nearby. Then you put your thumb and index finger around the one that caught your eye and tested for two things: If it was still really firm, it wasn't ripe enough. If the berry resisted when you pulled, it wasn't ripe enough, either. If you wanted a berry that would melt in your mouth, tasting of long summer days, warm from the sun, you had to find one that had lost its sheen—a berry that looked almost dusty and lackluster, one that practically fell apart in your hand. And you couldn't forget to include those tucked away or hanging down low where people forgot to look. They were everywhere. All you needed was to have the eyes to see.

On our last walk, we ate our way down the corridor and, fully sated, strolled hand-in-hand as we headed back to the car. It was there on that sun-kissed stretch where I realized that picking berries is a lot like dating. Often people forget that the commercialized image of the perfect pick has influenced what they're looking for and blinds them to seeing what is really and truly sweet fruit. In magazines, on book covers and in advertisements, the person of your dreams never has a receding hairline or an ounce of extra fat. The picture-perfect datable person has perfect teeth and is a runway model or someone famous. They never get the flu, have bad breath or have challenges at work. They don't fart and never have salad stuck in their teeth. He or she is never older or younger, of a different ethnic group or religion, and they certainly aren't divorced with kids.

When folks are mesmerized by the bright and shiny people, they miss those around them who are sweeter, fully ripened and ready for picking.

They look only at eye level in the picked-over branches. Time and again, those in the dating game reach for only the sour fruit—for those who are resistant to their advances. But if you look, there are people ripe and ready. They are everywhere. All you need is to have the eyes to see.

INTERNALIZED CHILDHOOD IMPRESSIONS
We form ideas about beautiful and ugly, desirable and undesirable through what we have overheard. We also

form our ideas from unspoken attitudes we have witnessed and the body language of those around us. Perhaps your pictures of the perfect body are in actuality the unexamined internalized ideas put together from a child's immature perspective. They include what you were exposed to, what you saw, smelled, felt and experienced. Sometimes your impression of a perfect body was formed by a toddler on a trip to the local supermarket. Here is just such an example from Shya's experience.

A "LEG'S-EYE" VIEW

I brushed my brow with the back of my hand in the mid-'80s as I jogged up 2nd Avenue on Manhattan's East Side. The August morning was already hot. It was going to be a scorcher. All in all, I liked the summer. Although it meant my daily run was more challenging, I liked the view. New York City streets, even in the early morning, were populated with other joggers, dog walkers and folks on their way to work. I saw many ladies wearing shorts and short skirts, showing lots of leg between the hem of their clothing and their sandals.

During my daily run to keep fit, my mind wandered and my eye roved. As I passed the buses and taxis, I found myself drawn to some legs and less drawn to others, but I didn't think much of it at first. I just enjoyed them. It was nice to stretch and exert myself, my legs pumping in rhythm as I sweated freely.

When I jogged past 43rd Street, my uptown momentum was momentarily interrupted by a red light, so I had the opportunity to notice a woman standing at the corner ahead of me. She had a great set of calves. In fact, they were "perfect." Jogging there in place, I suddenly flashed back to a time when I was a very small child.

My mother had taken me with her to the supermarket and I got lost. I didn't know where she was and I couldn't remember what she was wearing. I must have been really young because I recall crying while I ran from aisle to aisle, looking for my mother. I was so young that I was searching for her legs—that set of calves that represented safety and love, home and security. I was looking for those familiar calves that I knew to be my mommy's. I know now that I was never in any danger. I had simply wandered off and she was likely no more than a few feet away. But in my childish mind it was terrifying and my survival was at stake. I would be safe *only* if I could find those legs. I was not yet tall enough nor sophisticated enough to look for the whole person, so I was scanning from a leg's-eye view. I was surprised to find that all those years later, I still automatically scanned for a set of legs just like my mom's. I nodded to the gal as I passed her and continued on up the street.

9

WORKING TO BECOME
A BETTER YOU

*W*hen people have been single for a while, they often get to thinking that there's something wrong with them. That must be the reason no one has fallen in love with them yet. They think they need to be different somehow, a better version of themselves in order to attract a mate. Perhaps that's why you picked up this book, to discover how to improve yourself in order to get a relationship. Of course, this makes sense to your mind and its problem/solution way of functioning. But if you've spent your life trying to be different and better, then no doubt you've discovered that it doesn't work. Trying to be different doesn't make you happy or lead to successful relationships. We suggest that you already are the perfect version of you.

There is nothing to improve upon or make better. We suggest that being yourself while dating, expressing your truth and really listening to your date instead of trying to put on a show to impress is how you'll have the most fun. It's also how you can give yourself the best chance of meeting someone with whom you can ultimately have a Match Made in Heaven.

We'd like you to meet Madhu, an intelligent, attractive man of Indian descent in his mid-30s. Madhu had been proactively dating for many years, but always doubted that he was doing it right. He thought he needed to be a better version of himself in order to be attractive. As you read his story, see if you can let go of believing that you need to be a better you and notice how you are perfect just as you are.

JUST BE YOURSELF

As we settled into our seats in our living room across from Madhu, his belief that he was doing his life wrong and had to improve himself immediately became apparent. He clearly thought that he wasn't okay just as he was and believed that this was the reason that his dates weren't as successful as he hoped they would be.

"I'd like to know how I can reduce my shyness with women," he hurried, stumbling a little on his words in his eagerness. "When I'm on a date, sometimes I feel like the conversation runs out."

Madhu sat forward in his chair, his back straight and his hands on his knees, ready and primed for advice about how to improve himself and his dating skills. He looked at us, waiting for what he thought was coming.

"Get interested," Ariel replied and Shya nodded. "If you're worried about going somewhere or having the date be good, you won't be there with the gal in front of you. It sounds as if you're trying pretty hard to be interesting, but getting interested in her, listening to her is far more attractive. It isn't a problem if the conversation 'runs out' and you don't have anything 'interesting' to say. You could start with the truth. You could say something like, 'Wow, I feel tongue-tied and shy.' If you said that to me and we were on a date I'd find it very disarming. I might discover, 'Oh, me too! I'm feeling shy also.' You know, being honest is a really cool thing."

Madhu nodded, listening to Ariel's words and weighing

them in his mind. He was clearly interested in what she had to say, but at the same time, he wasn't quite convinced it was the answer he was looking for. It just didn't match the beliefs he already had about what he was doing wrong and how he might manipulate himself into doing things "right."

Shya joined in, "You know, people think they have to have it together," he said. "For the most part, people are living over top of their shyness, pretending they've got it together. All the pick-up lines you ever learned won't help in this situation."

At these words, a smile of recognition spread across Madhu's face and a little laugh escaped his lips. Shya had spotted one of his dating strategies, one of the ways he hid behind an act that he thought was better and more effective than just being himself.

"…And you've learned quite a few pick up lines, Madhu," he said.

Madhu laughed out loud. His eyes started to sparkle as he began to see the truth in what we were saying.

"Those lines are of absolutely no value," Shya went on. "What's valuable is to be with another person, to see what's there to be said. Say what you see, like: 'I find you attractive. Can we go out for coffee?' That's enough."

Madhu nodded. The idea of just being honest with a woman was clearly a completely new concept to him. His head tilted to one side and he kept nodding, caught between intrigue and disbelief.

Shya continued, "Or you could say, 'I don't know what to say. I feel like I want to be with you and yet I feel like I'm supposed to say deep and profound things and I just don't have any of those.' That would be okay."

Shya turned to Ariel with a smile. "Would that be okay if I said that to you? Would you still go out with me?" Ariel nodded and smiled back.

"She has to go out with me, though," Shya joked with a grin, "because she's married to me."

Ariel laughed with Shya and Madhu joined in. He had momentarily forgotten his "problem" and his dating agenda. In that moment he was simply having fun.

"Really, it's all about being available," Ariel said, "because, truthfully, the woman picks you."

"Huh?" Madhu said, not at all sure about this.

"Really," Shya said.

"Even online?" Madhu persisted, clearly confused about this entirely new concept and trying to figure out if he could believe it or not. His eyes darted from Ariel and Shya in turn, waiting for further explanation.

"I dated prior to the online thing," Ariel said. "But I have a feeling that if somebody wrote me a snappy pick-up line it would be much less attractive to me than if someone said something like 'I don't really know what to say here, this may not be the best expression of me but I'm attracted by your profile and I'd really like to meet you, or speak with you....' To me, I find an honest expression of yourself a whole lot more attractive than 'Hey baby...'"

"...If I could rearrange the alphabet I'd put U and I together," Madhu finished, supplying us with one of his pick-up lines.

Ariel's face dropped in mock-horror and Shya groaned, along with every member of the small audience we had in the room with us.

"That was an example of a bad one," Madhu laughed.

"Okay, give us an example of a good one then," Ariel said.

"Um, 'hello'?" Madhu said, still laughing. His "line" was simple, clear and direct. His face lit up as he suddenly saw the gift in just being himself.

"That might work," Ariel and Shya said in unison, laughing.

"I like that one a lot better," Shya said as Madhu and Ariel continued to laugh.

"You don't need a line," Ariel said. "You just need to be yourself."

"You don't need a line," Shya repeated. "You just need to be yourself."

It was a beautiful moment of Instantaneous Transformation and we all enjoyed it together.

HAVING AN AGENDA

Freshly invigorated, newly open to possibilities he'd never seen before, Madhu jumped in with another example from his dating life. "Just last week," he said, "I went on back-to-back dates. I thought they went okay, but then I got emails from both of the ladies telling me they didn't feel any chemistry. I felt like I didn't know how to generate something."

"Here's the thing," Shya said. "You're trying to get somewhere. You're not just allowing yourself to be with that other person. You want to score."

At this, the sudden smile of recognition slipped onto Madhu's face again and his eyes sparkled. "Right," he grinned.

"Well," Shya said, "try slowing it down so you're there with the other person. And you may discover you 'score' a lot more."

"The other thing is," Ariel added, "you don't have to 'generate' anything. I go back to what I first said: Get interested rather than be interesting."

Madhu nodded, remembering, absorbing her words.

"Listening is a brilliant way to be with someone," Shya said. "If you actually listen to them, they'll be very attracted to you. You can't do it as a technique, however, but if you actually listen, you become interesting."

Madhu smiled, gazing at Shya as he spoke. It was clear that he was really listening and experiencing transformation yet again as the words sunk in. He got it. In dating and in life, being yourself is the most attractive thing you can be.

"If you're interested," Shya concluded, "you become interesting."

"That's cool," Madhu said softly. "Thank you."

As we thanked him in turn we could see the dramatic shift in him. He was no longer perched at the edge of his seat, no longer stuck in his thoughts, no longer revising pick-up lines and adhering to agendas, no longer thinking he was doing it wrong and wondering how to do it right.

Now Madhu was relaxed. He was attractive and available. He had slowed down and stepped into the moment. In the inherent perfection of the present moment, he found that there was nothing he needed to do differently. There was no act he needed to perform to attract the opposite sex. He only had to be himself. He could listen to his date and that was enough. It was so much simpler than he had imagined when he sat down with us and his relief was a delight to behold.

 Just Be Yourself
TransformationMadeEasy.com/matchmadeinheaven

10

CHILDHOOD DECISIONS

*I*t's a challenge to just be yourself if you are still acting out a script that was written by you when you were a child. Each of us has made childish decisions that have greatly affected our abilities to relate as an adult. If you remember the example of Annina from an earlier chapter, she had decided that she was unattractive and that decision had blinded her to her own beauty.

Decisions that you make in your childhood run forward in time and play out in your adult life and your love relationships. Here is another example of how this works:

A very intelligent man named Terry comes to our seminars. Terry was smart enough to get a doctorate in history, but when he first attended our workshops, although he had an interest in dating, he wasn't at all adept. More at ease with his books than in social interactions, he didn't know how to bridge the gap between being interested in a lady and expressing that interest in a way that had women wanting to date him. He was self-conscious and, in the presence of women, he tended to get fidgety or nervous. We gently coached Terry to get involved wherever he was, to engage and listen. We often reiterated to him to "listen" with his eyes. In other words, we suggested that he look directly at whoever was speaking.

As Terry got better at listening in general, he naturally felt more at ease in the presence of a woman he found attractive. He became more socially adept and women began to reciprocate the interest he showed them. The less self-conscious he became the more he was able to express himself with humor and ease. Eventually Terry began dating Julie, an elegant woman in her early 40s. They really hit it off and when they sat together during our seminars, it was obvious from their body language that Terry and Julie were nurturing one another.

As their young relationship began to blossom, Terry looked more handsome. His body relaxed. Even his hair-cut appeared fresher, younger and more alive. However, much to our surprise, this fresh, crisp look that had naturally evolved didn't extend to the way Terry wore his clothes—even his new clothes. Let us describe it to you:

On any given Monday night, weekend seminar, or social event, Terry would walk in looking rather unkempt and his suits looked like they didn't really fit. Most noticeably, Terry's pants were cinched well below his waist, the seat of his trousers bagging down toward his knees and his shirts generally billowing out or becoming untucked. Terry's shirttails simply were not long enough to extend below the waist of his pants. Over a series of months, different people had gently tried to mention to him that perhaps he should pull up his pants. It was odd to see a professional man looking like a rap star in a music video or a teenager cruising the mall. Julie didn't want to pick on her new beau, but we could tell that privately, she was pleased when we had a conversation with Terry about his appearance.

It was a warm summer evening and our Monday Night Alive! seminar was well underway. People had arrived somewhat wilted from the intense heat of the day but by now, most had recovered in the cool of the air conditioning. The

two of us sat in the front of the room on our tall cush-
ioned chairs and Ariel said, "Okay, who else has something they want to talk about?"

Terry stood up and moved to the front of the room.
Standing stiffly with his legs apart, he looked braced
for battle, a stance we have come to recognize as one he
adopts when he feels uncomfortable. Terry was wearing a
white dress shirt with blue pin stripes, he had discarded
his suit jacket, and his blue and red tie was loosened,
slightly askew. His left shirttail hung out and the right
side billowed, his pants hanging low and loose below
his hips, the bottoms of his trousers pooling around his
shoes. And yet, his belt was tightened as if to highlight
the extra pounds around his middle. If you didn't know
Terry, you would never suspect that he was an accomplished man with a respectable position at work. You
certainly wouldn't take him for a man who rode miles
each day on his bike because he gave the appearance of
someone far removed from any type of physical activity.

"Hi, my name is Terry," he began, "and I want to talk
about my father coming to town. I haven't seen him in
about five years and he's on a lecture tour in Boston and
Washington, D.C. He's making a special trip to stop and
see me. I'm nervous about it."

This was a perfect moment, the moment we had been
waiting for. Sometimes we notice something about someone and then don't mention it for quite a while because
the timing isn't right. In Terry's case, we had always been
aware that while he's a mature, strong, accomplished
individual on the outside, he's tender inside. We hadn't
tried to mold him into a better, more respectable version
of himself because we didn't want to change him. But we
could see that his style raised eyebrows and had an impact on those around him. We could also see that Terry
was not aware of it, so we didn't address it until he made

himself available for the conversation.

Shya took the lead. "Well, Terry, if you really want to take care of your father and have an easy visit, there's one simple thing you can do that'll make a profound difference."

"What is it?" Terry asked.

"Pull up your pants."

Folks in the room chuckled as Terry looked down at his waist and then back at Shya. "I've been hearing that a lot lately," he said with a sheepish grin.

"Yes, Terry," Shya said, smiling kindly. "You adopted this style of dress as a teen in order to bug someone— likely your dad. I bet it got his attention."

"Yes, it did. My dad always had something to say about my clothes."

"I'm sure he did!" Shya said. Everyone laughed, including Terry.

"Kids need more than just food in order to grow and feel nourished," said Ariel. "They need attention, and many of us have learned that negative attention is better than no attention at all. Because our parents were so often distracted, our young minds devised ways to get them to notice us. As a result, those immature ways of relating follow us into life.

"We once met a lady who got attention from her parents by eating a piece of food that had spoiled. She got food poisoning and had to go to the emergency room. By the time she was in her 30s, she had been hospitalized with food poisoning more than a dozen times. This destructive method of getting her parents' attention had become a lifestyle."

"Terry," Shya said, "unbeknownst to you, this simple childhood decision is really affecting your life today. I'm sure your girlfriend is happy that we're talking about this because she hasn't wanted to say anything, even though it's been bothering her."

Julie nodded with a compassionate smile. As the two of them locked eyes, we could see that Terry felt seen and loved, but not judged—even by himself.

"Let's talk about work for a moment," Ariel said. "I know that you're looking for a higher paid position. If I were to read your resume, Terry, I would be very impressed. But if I saw you dressed as you are, and I had a candidate of similar caliber to you, I would hire that other individual. What you have been promoting with your pants style is not the competent man that you are."

Terry looked down at his waist again and back up with a grin as he grasped his waistband and tugged it upward. "Yes," he replied, "I get it."

"Really, Terry," Shya said kindly, "if you take care of this one thing, it will make the visit with your father much easier."

"Also," Ariel said, "it's time to stop looking at what he can do for you. You can stop thinking of him as being your 'dad,' as someone whose attention you need, as someone you need to impress or need something from. As an adult, I look at what I can do to take care of my parents, not because they need taking care of. They are not infirm but this is how I take care of everyone in my life, including my folks. Shya and I look to see what our environment 'requests.'"

Pausing, Ariel took a breath and a moment to regroup. Taking care of people and things in our environment is an important concept and she wanted to do her best to communicate the ideas in a way that made sense to Terry.

"Let's see if I can make this concept easier to grasp," she said. "Here's another example, Terry. Our friend Caitlin, a costume designer, was working on a small independent film. Since a lot of the film crew were more inexperienced than she was, she realized that she could either just 'do her job,' or she could take care of those around her.

"On one occasion she helped the driver of the wardrobe truck because he hadn't driven in New York City before. He didn't realize that there were bridges and parkways where a truck wasn't permitted. Caitlin wrote him a list of things he needed to know, which he kept on his dashboard.

"On another occasion someone at the catering truck dropped a case of strawberries on the floor. Caitlin helped him pick up the berries. It wasn't technically her job but she had the time and she saw that it needed to be done. Taking care of your environment includes looking around to see what needs your attention. But in your case, it also includes taking care of your dad by not purposefully dressing in a way that is geared to bother him."

Terry nodded. He had grown thoughtful. His stance had relaxed and he was now standing with ease.

"Thank you!" Terry said as he moved to his seat. "Thank you both, and thank you all very much."

Two weeks later, Terry's father, Joseph, came to one of our Monday seminars while he was in town. When Terry introduced us to Joseph, an athlete, we saw that Shya's initial assessment of Terry's sloppy fashion statement had been extremely accurate. Terry had been dressing poorly to bother his dad. Meeting his father allowed another piece of the 'Terry puzzle' to fall into place. Terry is actually quite fit, although you never would have known it from his baggy drawers tightened too low on his waist, which highlighted those extra pounds. How better to bother a demanding father than to appear slovenly? How better to assert your independence than to be soft and round when your father prizes fitness?

Terry had put together a strategy in adolescence and pre-pubescence that he had carried into his adult life.

Now, as he began to see himself without judging what he saw, he became himself rather than a statement against his father. Soon, when he walked into a room full of people, they were drawn to his smile and his face rather than his shirttails and baggy behind. Easily and rather effortlessly, his excess weight melted away so that his trim figure reflected his level of fitness rather than disguising it. As he let go of trying to be independent of his father, he was able to manifest the athlete that had been hidden under those extra pounds.

It was truly a pleasure to watch as Terry moved on in his life and in his relationship. He is no longer fettered by the decisions of a young boy to bother his father and to assert his "independence" by being "not like" his dad.

11

IF MAMA AIN'T HAPPY, AIN'T NOBODY HAPPY

REPEATING PARENTAL PATTERNS

In Costa Rica, during one of our winter immersion courses into the magic of Instantaneous Transformation, we met with a number of participants and recorded video mini-sessions of the interactions. One afternoon, we sat down with Shea, a young man from Minnesota. We had known Shea for a couple of years and had met his girlfriend, Ali, a few months before. It was clear to us that Shea was attempting to build a relationship without actually paying attention to how he related.

Shea's dating experience was limited. His ideas of what constituted a "good" relationship were largely an amorphous, foggy theory based loosely on concepts he had been exposed to while reading, or in discussions with other young people. But unbeknownst to him, Shea was also acting out the cultural script which had been written when he was a youngster. As he was starting on his journey toward having a Match Made in Heaven, he'd been filling in the gaps in his knowledge and experience with youthful theories and reasonable facsimiles of what he had been exposed to as a child. The familiar dynamics of how a man and woman should relate, as seen in Shea's family, had been internalized and largely unexamined up until this point.

It was a bright sunny day and the verdant hills could be seen behind Shea, the foliage lush and tropical. His straight brown hair was parted neatly on the left side, the brown of his brows arched in a perfect line above his glasses. He was wearing a dark pink polo shirt which complemented the blush of his cheeks and youthful appearance. During our interaction, Shea began to see what was written on the pages of his familial script. He was discovering how to be himself rather than blindly following in the footsteps of those who came before.

He began to speak in an earnest manner, and while he tried to collect his thoughts and express himself, his eyes darted off to the side as if reading words he had prepared. "In intimate relationships," he said, "how can I distinguish if I'm living my life on my own terms and not on the terms of my girlfriend?"

Ariel jumped right in. "Well, you haven't been living life on your terms, as you put it, so far. You've been caving in to the whims of the woman you're with and letting her lead you when she doesn't even know where she's going."

"Yes," Shea replied emphatically. It was likely he could think of plenty of examples of this type of behavior on both their parts. Yet it was obvious that this was not where he wanted to be in his relationship, nor how he wanted to behave. He breathed in and released a barely audible sigh. Then, the next question slowly began to emerge. Shea had quickly identified the way he had been relating as a problem. Now he wanted to know how to change things, how to be better, or how to do things differently.

"So how...?" he began.

"Well, look at it this way, Shea," Shya interjected,

stopping the forward momentum of Shea's urge to work on himself. "Do you know what you want in a relationship?"

After a slight of pause, Shea said, "Yes," once again. But this time his response was a tad less emphatic.

"And what might that be?" Shya asked.

Shea's reply was unexpected. We thought he might say something like, "I want to get married," or "I want to be happy," or "I want to stop fighting with Ali." But his answer, while reasonable enough on the surface, sounded like he had lifted it from a text written by an adolescent—a juvenile's prescription superimposed on reality. Shea spoke as if he were an actor in a grade school production reciting the words to a play. The phrases came out stilted, in fits and starts, as he struggled to keep from forgetting his lines.

He stammered, "I want to support and be supported in a gentle and genuine and honest way...and have honest, loving communication ...with another human being."

It took us a moment to respond because his answer showed us that he was not looking at his relationship with Ali at all. The fact that he was living with this young lady, already sharing his life and his home, was nowhere in his awareness in that moment. When Shya had asked Shea what he wanted in a relationship, Shea had stepped out of the moment. He had not looked at his truth in that instant, but instead had fallen back into a prewritten script. In this way, he didn't have to sit in the discomfort of not knowing. He didn't have to be unsure or feel like a novice at relating. He could, in effect, pull the blanket of a theory over his head and then he would no longer have to be there. His concept would stand there instead.

"Well, it starts with you," Shya eventually replied. "You can't control whether or not Ali is gentle and genuine with supportive, loving communications. Those are broad concepts, Shea."

"Right," he replied earnestly, the tip of his tongue moistening his lips.

"But if you're not being honest," Shya continued, "you can't expect honesty in return. For example, if something is said or done that doesn't feel good to you, and you suppress yourself—either for fear of losing her or for fear of her getting angry with you and the consequences you'll have to deal with—pretty soon the threat of her getting upset determines how you're going to interact. In other words, as it stands now, if your girlfriend threatens to be upset, you behave."

"Right," he said nodding. Shya had perfectly described the dynamic that had developed between Shea and Ali.

"Plenty of relationships go just like that for a lifetime," Ariel continued. She didn't want him to misconstrue the conversation in a way that would lead to the inaccurate conclusion that if Ali was managing him via threat of upset, this was a "bad" thing. In a Transformational Approach to Dating, Relating and Marriage, it's important to keep treating what you discover about yourself and your relationship in a nonjudgmental manner.

MANAGING BY THREAT OF UPSET

Shea and Ali's way of relating was not unusual. Many people suppress their truth for fear of losing their mate or to avoid having to deal with a temper tantrum. Plenty of folks manipulate those around them by threatening to get upset if things don't go the way they want or if they don't get their way.

"Dominating by threatening to get upset or not being truthful," said Shya, "and then blaming your partner for your lack of honesty is one 'normal' possibility in relationship."

"We recently saw an example of this way of relating,"

Ariel added. "Shya and I lead courses at the New Yorker Hotel in Manhattan and we get a hotel room there when we do our weekend workshops. The last time we were there, we saw a couple in their mid-to-late 60s, staying in the hotel room next door to ours. One morning as we exited our room, they happened to be leaving their room also. The woman came out first and marched down the hall while the man trailed behind in a fog. Once she reached the elevator, she repeatedly jabbed the button, as if to advertise her complaint that they were late and he was slow and to blame. She picked on him all the way down in the elevator.

"I saw the two of them again the night we were leaving the hotel after our workshop was over. They had on different clothes, were going to a different destination but the dynamic was the same. It appeared that she was taking him someplace else and he trailed behind her like her child. At the curb, she hailed a cab while he stood there, slightly removed physically, and totally removed in his mind. I see that as a possibility for you, Shea. You could easily get married and go through life with this theme playing in your relationship."

"Yeah, that sounds like the opposite of what I want," Shea replied.

"Well, it's interesting you say that, Shea," Shya said. "Because if you're getting the opposite of what you want, then you're resisting something."

Again, this is a law of physics as well as the First Principle of Instantaneous Transformation. For every action, there is an equal and opposite reaction. Or what you resist persists and grows stronger. If Shea was behaving in a way opposite to his true heart's desire, he was probably trying to not be like one or the other of his parents. It was time to find out.

"So who are you trying to not be like?" Ariel asked.

"Yes," Shya repeated, "who are you trying to not be like? Who in your family ruled?"

Shea's eyes bounced to his script once more. He looked at what he assumed to be true but he didn't actually look. "My dad," he replied with a slight smile, giving himself and us the answer he thought we wanted.

"Really?" Shya said, challenging him to look deeper.

Suddenly, something totally new appeared in Shea's face as he saw the reality of how his parents interacted. "Actually..." He paused as pictures of his parents spilled out of his memory, replacing his well-worn script with a refreshing clarity.

"Yes?" Shya prompted.

Shea gave a slight laugh. He was not fully prepared for his truth, but there it was nonetheless. He looked up once again to grab the words from the script. But this time, Shea recited the words of his dad.

"My father always said, 'If Mama ain't happy, ain't nobody happy.'"

You could see Shea's mixed emotions as his truth showed up—pleasure at seeing things honestly, followed closely by his judgments of himself and of his dad.

"Yes," Shya said, "that's right. You've modeled yourself after your parents' relationship."

"Uh-huh," he said.

"You're behaving like your dad," Ariel said, "and picking someone to manage you by threat of upset, just like your mom did."

"Did I ever tell you the story of Jake and Becky and the chicken soup?" Shya asked.

"It doesn't ring a bell," Shea said.

"Oh, that's good. I can tell you now." Shya settled back in his chair and began to tell his tale.

CHICKEN SOUP

"There once was a couple, Jake and Becky. Every Friday night, Becky made chicken soup and every Friday night, her husband Jake would say, 'Becky, this chicken soup is great, but it's not as good as my mother's. My mother must have had a special ingredient that she put in because even though this is a great chicken soup, it's not as good as my mother's.'

"Over the years, Becky continued to try and make the soup to his taste. She used different recipes, but she always got a similar response: 'You know, Becky, this chicken soup is really great, but it's not as good as my mother's.'

"One day, Becky was doing the laundry when the washing machine broke down. The suds overflowed the laundry room and she got lost in cleaning it up. It was a Friday, the chicken soup was on the stove, and while she was dealing with the mess, the soup burned. It was too late to go out and get fresh vegetables and fresh chicken, so Becky couldn't start again. Ultimately, she just served the chicken soup, quickly placing the bowl in front of Jake. Then she walked back into the kitchen, hoping he wouldn't notice.

"But suddenly she heard, 'Becky, get in here! This chicken soup...!'

"She expected to be berated for ruining his meal, but much to her surprise Jake said, 'This is the best! This is *just* like my mother used to make!'"

Delighted, Shea began to laugh.

"See, that's the best," Shya said. "What Jake grew up with was the best. What you grew up with was the role model for a successful relationship and that's what love looks like to you. So you look to create the same type of relationship that your parents had, whether you realize it or not. But you're recreating a relationship where your

mother led by threat of upset and your father played out
the role of being a victim to a dominating woman. This
dynamic in their relationship happened because that's
what they grew up with—and so it goes from generation
to generation. In my story, Jake had come to associate his
mother's soup with love. Since his mother always burned
the chicken soup when he was a child, that's what he
looked for when he grew up. Our minds fold in extra
things that don't make for a satisfying relationship if we
try to emulate them. Do you see?"

"Yes," Shea replied. He had relaxed into himself and
now he was looking rather adult, handsome and at ease.

"You've built your schematic for a loving relationship
based on a fight between your mom and dad," said Shya.
"And in this scenario, your dad apparently lost and your
mom won."

"But in truth," Ariel pointed out, "your dad wasn't the
victim of your mom. He let her win because then he
could abdicate responsibility for his own life."

"Just like you've been doing, Shea," Shya said. "Then
you don't have to be responsible. If something doesn't
turn out, it's not your fault."

It was as if a light bulb abruptly lit up in Shea's brain
as pieces of our conversation suddenly fit into place. In
Ariel's story about the couple at the hotel, the wife had
looked unreasonable and the man looked like her victim.
Shea's dad's statement, "If Mama ain't happy, ain't nobody happy," had painted a picture of his mother as the
one who was unreasonable and to blame for unpopular
decisions. It was a roundabout way of saying, "I don't
agree, but I'm just going along with her to avoid her
wrath. Please don't be mad at me."

"Yeah. Wow!" Shea said, suddenly coming alive.

"Here's the thing," Shya continued. "How you've been
acting is a covert way of being right. You let your girl-

friend fail to prove your point of view rather than just staying strong in yourself and saying, 'No, that's not going to work. We're doing it my way.'"

"What was it your father said?" Ariel asked.

"If Mama ain't happy, ain't nobody happy," Shea replied with a smile.

"Guess who got to look good in that one?" Ariel asked.

This time Shea's answer was his truth. "My dad. Wow!" he exclaimed as he tossed out his old misconceptions.

"When your mother made a mistake, whose fault was it?" Shya asked.

"My dad's," Shea replied.

"No, in your dad's eyes, the mistakes are *her* fault, Shea. Quietly, surreptitiously, he thinks that if they had done things his way, it would have turned out differently. Your father succumbs to your mother's wishes and if things turn out negatively, he can put the blame on her. Then he doesn't have to take any responsibility."

"There's a possibility, Shea," Ariel said, "for true partnership between you and Ali. You haven't grown up in it, but there is the possibility of it. One of the things it takes to be in partnership is honesty. If something doesn't sit right with you, speak up. If Shya let me get away with things that didn't sit right with him, I'd end up looking silly to myself or to other people. I'd do things that would be damaging to myself, to him, to others and to my relationship."

Shya added, "This dynamic goes both ways. Ariel is honest with me as well. She doesn't let things slip by either. Letting your partner 'get away' with things is a 'normal' relationship. But you can easily have a relationship that is exceptional."

"Part of operating in partnership," said Ariel, "has to do with making sure that we're really honest with each other, nothing held back. We don't go to sleep with resentments. Actually, in the early days, even though I never wanted to go to sleep with resentments, it was a challenge. It was as if I had to prompt myself to speak up in order to get past a reticence to speak. It was important that we didn't wait to communicate until we were angry enough to bypass our internal governor, the anger driving what needed to be said.

When you say things in anger, even if they're true, you hurt your partner in the process.

"These days, we don't have to make a decision or be vigilant in order to make sure that things are good between us. It's just a natural flow where I can count on him to have my back," Ariel said with a grin, "and to have my front, my sideways, and up and down and every way and vice versa."

"Yes," Shea said, smiling and nodding wisely. "Partnership sounds better than burnt chicken soup."

We all chuckled.

"Thank you so much," Shea said with a smile. "That's so cool!"

"You're welcome," we replied.

If Mama Ain't Happy, Ain't Nobody Happy
TransformationMadeEasy.com/matchmadeinheaven

12

BEING THE AUTHOR
OF YOUR LIFE

*I*n our first book devoted to the theme of relating, *How to Create a Magical Relationship*, we introduced the term, "relationship splitter." Relationship splitting is such a disruptive influence on otherwise healthy relationships that we devoted an entire section of that book to exploring many of the ways this dynamic can manifest.

In short, relationship splitting is a behavior that is first seen among children and their parents, and it expands into later life. A relationship splitter is a person who has a specific type of incompletion with his or her parents. He or she has usually bonded with the parent of the opposite sex to the exclusion of the other. In early childhood, this behavior may be seen as cute. It can be sweet to see a young boy who is so attentive to his mother or a young girl who loves to be with her daddy. But if the competition with your parent for your mother or father's affection and attention continues into adulthood, it becomes a way of relating that automatically disrupts or destroys all the relationships it comes into contact with.

There are numerous anecdotes in that book that demonstrate the different ways a relationship splitter acts, how to recognize the phenomena and how to neutralize its effects on your relationship. But what happens when you discover that *you* split relationships? What happens when you are the person who is so locked into competing with your mother (or father if you are a man) that you automatically compete with all other women around you? This is what happened to Anne.

MANAGING YOURSELF

Anne is a European beauty—tall, lean, creamy skin, long dark hair that cascades down her back, an engaging smile. She could have been a model if she had chosen that as a profession. It was easy to appreciate Anne's good looks but not so easy for the women around her to tolerate how attentive she was to their boyfriends and husbands. Although Anne was unaware of it at first, virtually all of her conversations with people during our seminars were with men who were already attached to someone else. She had an uncanny ability to sit next to only those men who were in a relationship, while leaving the seats next to the available men vacant. If there was an exercise that required a partner, rarely if ever would you see Anne with a woman or a single guy—she would always pair up with a man who was married or in a committed relationship. For the most part, men were unaware that they were pawns in her ongoing war with her mother. They just enjoyed the seemingly spontaneous attention given to them by such a lovely lady.

Anne joined us for one of our winter Instantaneous Transformation immersion courses in Costa Rica. During the week that she was in this tropical environment where it was common to wear lightweight attire, her way of moving, acting and interacting with others seemed to be highlighted.

One day in the course room, Anne's competitive nature was brought up. In a very gentle manner, people discussed with Anne her ways of relating so that she could become aware of them. It was a challenge for her to not judge herself for her behavior, but she did a rather remarkable job. As she looked at how she behaved without resisting what she observed and without judging herself, this way of relating dropped away so that married and single men and women alike could all enjoy her company. It was Instantaneous Transformation.

However, as with many well-entrenched behaviors, her relationship-splitting ways began to re-emerge over time. When she attended a weekend workshop with us the following summer, she had fallen back into some of her old familiar ways. This was upsetting news to Anne. She wanted transformation to be a magic pill. She wanted to see her competitive, relationship-splitting behavior and then have it be over with once and for all—but it doesn't work that way. She hadn't realized that transformation happens in an instant, but it is also cumulative. It's a lifestyle of bringing awareness to how you live your life without judging what you see. Transformation is not a one-time event. If you see something without judging it, it's enough. In that moment, it's over. (This is the Third Principle of Instantaneous Transformation). If the habit shows up again, if you see it again without judging it, it's over then, too.

During the seminar that weekend, Anne was dismayed by the news that she was not "over" her old familiar ways. It took courage on her part to look, see and let go. In the following weeks, Anne had questions about how to manage her tendency to automatically compete with the women around her and so she contacted us.

She is a member of *The Premium Excellence Club,* our online subscription program where participants sign up to receive a video mini-session of us working with someone each week in their email inbox. The videos that formed the basis for *How to Have a Match Made in*

Heaven were all originally released as part of this program. Another feature of *The Premium Excellence Club* is the Question and Answer section. Each month members write in their questions and we publish one or more of the questions and our answer. We sent Anne our answer in advance of publication and she was moved to write back. The email exchange was so powerful that we got her permission to publish it in its entirety.

Below is the question Anne submitted to *The Premium Excellence Club*, our reply and the ensuing email exchange. If you pay attention, you will see how she moved from being the victim of her mechanical behaviors into being the author of her life. She starts by equating her competitive nature to an incurable disease and she ends up being excited to see the nuances of how her mechanics manifest themselves. In effect, she becomes inspired as she sees herself honestly, as opposed to being disheartened and feeling sorry for herself. We can all learn a lot from Anne, her courage and her journey.

ANNE'S PREMIUM EXCELLENCE CLUB QUESTION:

Hi Ariel and Shya!

Regarding being in competition with women: You recently told me at a workshop, "You will have to manage this." This sentence goes around and around in my head, as I am not sure what you mean by "managing." I thought transformation was supposed to be easy and as long as I see my competition and keep looking, without judging, it will resolve itself.

I guess the way I interpret the word "managing" is that my behavior is similar to a disease with no cure. I have to live with it and be careful not to hurt anybody. I find myself working on myself and on this "topic" and not trusting myself because I suddenly think that simply seeing it is not enough. Could you give me some clarification on this?

Thank you! Anne

OUR ANSWER:

Dear Anne,

There is a paradox here. Transformation is instantaneous but the effects of living a transformational lifestyle are also cumulative over time. You can transform in an instant, but that is revocable in an instant if you close your eyes to how you are behaving and go back to your old mechanical ways.

Transformation happens in a state of honesty: a nonjudgmental seeing of something as it is. It is clear from your question that you are judging what you see and actually, you have an agenda to see your competitive nature with women in order to get rid of it. This is actually the First Principle of Instantaneous Transformation in disguise: What you resist (secretly try to change/avoid seeing because you think it's bad) will persist and grow stronger.

If you suddenly made a fortune and didn't know what to do with the money and we told you that you would have to learn how to manage your wealth, you would not see this as the same as having an incurable disease! Thinking of your unaware, competitive nature with other women as a disease is a slight judgment, don't you think?

During the workshop, unbeknownst to you, you were once again flirting and attempting to attract those men who were already in a relationship, while ignoring the women in the room and those men who were eligible. When we gently pointed it out to you, you did not treat this as good news. You became upset and said something to the effect of, "I thought I was over that!" But if you've had a life strategy in place from childhood of competing with your mother and then, by extension, competing with women in relationship, this has become a well-ingrained habit that you will need to manage. When you are feeling centered in yourself and aware of your environment and your impact upon it, you are less likely to exclude women and try to get the attention of men in relationship. When you are off-center in yourself or feeling insecure, or if you are currently fighting with your mom, for instance, you are more likely to fall back into your old habit of competition.

To manage this, take an active interest in how you are relating with those around you as an indicator of whether you are centered—acting in a creative, proactive manner—as opposed to putting on blinders when you're upset, out of sorts or acting out an old script put in place by an adolescent version of yourself.

Embedded in your question is a complaint that transformation doesn't really work, because you saw your competitive nature once—so that should be enough to handle it for all time. You want your competitive behavior to be over with. You want to take the "magic transformation pill" and never have to look at or be responsible for your behavior again. That is not transformation. That is change.

Transformation is not an achievement. It is a lifestyle.

Warmly,

Ariel and Shya

WE RECEIVED THIS REPLY VIA EMAIL:

Dear Ariel, Dear Shya,

Thank you for taking time and answering my question! The different aspects of your answer are very helpful.

When I first read the part where you described that you saw me flirting and trying to attract men in a relationship during the workshop, I got upset again. It felt like you were speaking about another person.

Then later on that day I went swimming at the lake and ran some errands, studying my own culture in regards to my behavior around men and women. And what I discovered was rather surprising: During my shopping trip, for instance, I would see a guy that I felt attracted to and a moment later a woman came around the corner that turned out to be his girlfriend or wife. Or I was waiting for the train and saw another man that I felt interested in and shortly after I saw that he was with a woman, too. This happened a few times over the course of the afternoon!

On the other hand, I could in fact see that I was sometimes intentionally ignoring the men who were there by themselves—not in all, but in some cases.

This whole topic feels a lot lighter now. There are still judgments in there, because I always used to have an idea about myself, how I am in that respect, and now I am discovering new things that I would not have expected to find. I can see how much I wanted to be over it already and this stopped me from staying awake and continuing to look.

Love, Anne

OUR RESPONSE:

Dear Anne,

Very, very cool! Isn't it neat to see that you are automatically tuned in on men in relationship and it isn't even something you think about, or plan! You didn't even see the lady until she rounded the corner or, secondarily, see the woman who was standing right there. That really is cool because now you don't have to blame yourself. It is simply something to pay attention to and to compensate for. Seeing it places you in control of your life rather than being the victim of repeating circumstances. We are really happy for you!

Sending kind wishes from our vacation in Oregon,
Ariel and Shya

Dear Ariel, Dear Shya!

Thanks for your note. Yes, it is very cool (-: And I keep seeing new things—meanwhile, I can even have a sense of humor when I see what I am actually doing.

I really enjoyed the picture of you, Ariel, and your sisters on Facebook! I find the lady in the middle looks very similar to you.

Today, I was resting in my hammock while listening to the True Love podcast on your *Being Here* radio show. I was really inspired by it. I am so grateful for your radio shows—thank you so much for doing them every week. It's such a treat.

Hugs! Anne

13

CHILDHOOD DECISIONS
BRING ADULT COMPLICATIONS

*I*n this section we will meet a very lovely German lady in her mid-40s by the name of Christiane. She was raised by a father who has some very strong prejudices that most of us would find repugnant. During World War II, he was a Nazi sympathizer and he still is strongly biased against those who come from a Jewish background. By today's standards, Christiane would be well justified for having resisted him. But her acts of defiance and "revenge" against his small-minded nature have had devastating results on this beautiful woman with a very big heart.

Join us as we sit down with her and discuss the art of being compassionate. It was a surprisingly light-hearted conversation, given the weighty nature of some of the things we talked about. And yet, with a transformational perspective, even deeply charged and emotional subjects can be treated respectfully, yet lightly.

COMPASSION BEGINS AT HOME
Christiane has ash blond shoulder-length hair, parted in the middle, that frames her face with light curls. She is elegant and articulate and when she met with us, her marriage was deeply troubled. As we sat in an outdoor

area near a hotel in Hamburg, the day was breezy and the flowers behind Christiane and the wall of ivy behind the two of us danced in the wind.

Christiane gathered her thoughts, and as she began to talk, she got right to the point. She said, "Lately—no, not lately. Since 17 years, I'm trying to make my husband understand me and now I'm trying to make my daughter understand me."

We decided to quickly get to the point as well. Christiane mistakenly thought that her discord was with her husband and daughter. What she didn't realize was that the "fight" dynamic had been set in place by an early version of herself. Old vendettas and ways of relating to her primary love relationship, her father, were now being played out in all the relationships in her life.

Like an adult who has a big surprise for a young person, Shya practically sang, "I've got something for you-oo."

"I am so sure you have!" she said with a chuckle.

"Night before last, we were at dinner after the workshop and you said something that was really, really telling."

"Yes," Ariel continued. "It really grabbed our attention."

Like a young child caught in a game, Christiane laughed and covered her mouth with one hand. She had an idea about the subject we were going to raise. Actually, we're fairly sure that it was not by chance that she raised that topic at dinner.

Christiane had sat at our table to have a meal after a workshop we had led in Hamburg. The restaurant was packed with participants from the weekend who had gotten together to extend the time we all spent with one another. Sitting at a table with several other friends and acquaintances, Christiane managed to tell us some very intimate details about her life in that casual setting.

"You know, chatting with you really gave me insights into your life, Christiane," Shya said. "See, you think you're at war with your husband. But I think you're at war with your father."

"Yes," she said in a sober manner.

"This war with your father just transfers over to your husband."

"Yes, yes!" Christiane exclaimed as she saw the truth of Shya's statement.

"You told us that you have four children and that they all have Jewish first and middle names."

Christiane nodded with a knowing smile.

"You told us that you gave them Jewish names because it bothers your father who was 16 at the time when Hitler came to power. According to you, he still tells anti-Semitic jokes that are unkind. And you always fight with him about that. But you really got him back when you picked out the names for your children."

Christiane couldn't help herself. She grinned broadly.

"And when you told us all about this, you were happy," Ariel continued. "You were gleeful. You were very excited about it. And now, you're really happy because your daughter, Leah, is dating a Jewish boy and that is like heaven."

"Yes, that is even better!" she said.

While she was listening to what we had to say so far, Christiane went through a myriad of emotional states: guilty, gleeful, slightly embarrassed, a touch nervous, anticipatory, proud of herself and slightly confused. Again, it was obvious to us that she had come to the recording session to untangle the dynamic with her husband and daughter and to handle her relationship with her father.

"The things you revealed over dinner give me the schematic," said Shya, "the framework, the paradigm, the system through which you're looking at life. Your lifelong agenda is to prove to your father that he's wrong."

"Yes, that is my revenge to him," she said. In that moment, Christiane's face suddenly appeared angry, sullen and hard.

"I find it interesting that that emotion came up when you said the word 'revenge,'" Shya said, directing Christiane's attention back to herself and to what she was feeling.

"Giving your children Jewish names is your revenge against him," he continued. "The only problem with that is that although you may be unaware of it, you're transferring that revengeful way of relating to your relationship. I know you don't want that, because you want to have a peaceful marriage. You want him to want to be with you. But if you do the same things you've been doing since you were a child to prove your father wrong about how he's lived his life, you'll be taking that same stance with your husband, Claudio. You will devote yourself to proving that Claudio is doing his life 'wrong,' just like your father. There is no peace in that.

"Christiane, your father could not have done his life any differently than he did. If we put ourselves in his situation, with his background and conditioning during that time in the history of this country, we might have done the same thing."

"And resisting his viewpoint only reinforces it," Ariel said.

Christiane remained unconvinced. In her mind, her father was wrong—absolutely wrong. It was an immutable fact. She had proof—proof she had gathered over a lifetime of collection. She assumed we would find him as repugnant as she did. He was a *Nazi* after all.

Shya tried a different tack to defuse Christiane's fight with her father. He said, "Ariel and I were once in Bavaria, where we visited a friend of ours named Dolma. We met Dolma when we lived together at a meditation center in Italy for a couple of years. When she moved, she invited us to come and spend some time with her. She was living outside Munich on a dairy farm and the farmer and his wife lived downstairs. Upstairs were rooms that they rented out to tourists and that was where we stayed.

"Uh-hum," Christiane said, nodding, not sure where this was leading.

"One night, the farmer and his wife invited us down to the cozy parlor in their home. He played a little concertina and we drank wine and we danced. Then he stopped and said to me, 'I am so sorry.'

"I said, 'For what? You did nothing wrong.'

"He said, 'Yes, I was a Nazi during the war.'

"The farmer looked at me expectantly, anticipating that I would judge him as harshly as he did himself. Even though I come from a Jewish background myself and am well versed in the horrors of the war, I didn't have it in me to be unkind to this man. He was old and heartsick and had obviously been punishing himself enough. I said, 'So?'

"Taking a deep breath, relieved to be unburdening himself, the farmer said, 'Let me tell you about it.'

"He told us that one day, the Nazis came to his village and said to the villagers, 'All the men will meet at the town square at 6 o'clock in the morning tomorrow. And if you don't show up, we are going to come to your home and kill you and your entire family.' The farmer had no choice."

Christiane's face softened as she saw this man's dilemma. But she still wasn't ready to cut her father any slack. "Uh-hum," she said.

"This man had to become a Nazi or they would have killed his family. He told us that his brother had died on the Russian front. When he got back home, he found that both his parents had been killed in his absence and among his family he was the sole survivor of the war. His whole life had been destroyed and he was asking *me* to forgive *him*. Our hearts went out to him. He had had absolutely no choice.

"As children, Christiane, we judge our parents as though they should be different than they are. But your father could not have been different than he was. The circumstances of his life, the whole social order at that time, sucked him up like a tornado and he had absolutely no control over his life. He had to do that and he probably felt he was being patriotic. In truth, Christiane, punishing him for how he was when he had no other choice in his life, actually punishes you."

"Let's look at the impact your fight with your father has had on your relationship to your husband, Claudio," Ariel said. "You visit the same type of judgments and mental schematics on him. We've met Claudio and he is very easily pushed into being stubborn about a point of view. You can actually push him into opposing you, just for the sake of being contrary. There are times when you're harmonious, but there are times when you're really fighting. I also believe that the fighting happens because that's what you look for in a love relationship. Your primary love relationship, your relationship with your father, is a fight."

"Yes, it is," she said, nodding tightly.

"It would be wise to forgive your father, Christiane, for what he couldn't have done any differently than he did, and forgive yourself for the way you have interacted with him," Shya continued. "'Forgive' means to give up the right to punish, to act as though the offense never happened. It also means giving up the *desire* to punish as well. You need to have some compassion for yourself first."

The concept of forgiveness was all well and good, but Christiane wasn't ready to lay down the fight just yet. She still had to see how she justified her anger and resentment. She hadn't fully comprehended how much she took pride and satisfaction in being right and her father being wrong, and how much she felt it was her job to point out the error of his ways.

We know few words in the German language, but one of them is *schadenfreude*. *Schadenfreude* is the pleasure one derives from the discomfort or misfortunes of others. It is when you are gloating or happy that someone is suffering. Christiane was so at war with her dad that her *schadenfreude* was plain to see. But what Christiane had not yet seen was that she was not the opposite of her father. In fact, she was just like him. While he was programmed by his culture to hate Jews, she hated him and those like him with equal vehemence. The object of their hatred was different but the hatred itself was the same. In resisting him, she had become him.

"If you want to create harmony in your relationship, you have to tell the truth about how much you enjoy bothering your father, because you do," Ariel said. "When we talked with you the other night, you were delighted when you told us about your children's names and the effect it had on your dad."

"Yes. Somehow, I have the impression I have the right to punish him," Christiane admitted, "although I know that it's not true."

"You do have the right to punish him. You can do it," Ariel said. "But there are definitely consequences."

Christiane's face became stormy. She looked young and upset—petulant.

"Yeah, well," she said defensively, "I think my father punished me when I was young. He always took my brother's side. My brother always came first. I had always to stand back. I wasn't very important in my family."

"But you're still blaming him for that." Ariel said.

Shya asked, "How old were you when you became angry with him for that?"

"I think I've been angry since my brother was born."

"Oh, I'm sure you were," Shya replied with certainty.

"Yeah, okay. I was two years old."

"That's right. So you're still in a temper tantrum—the temper tantrum of a two-year-old. And you're going to make your father pay for being happy that he had a son, when in this culture, having a son was something he was trained to want. Your father was following the dictates of the culture, that a son is important and daughters are less so. That is cultural. That is what he grew up with. That is what his whole training was. And you think he should be more sensitive, more compassionate than he knows how to be.

"My darling, compassion begins at home. You have to learn to be more compassionate and then it might happen for him, too. He is never going to change, but you do have the possibility to transform. If you allow him to be the way he is, without punishing him for his attitudes, it is possible that your relationship will transform. One thing for sure is that if you stop punishing him, you'll be far happier in yourself."

"I feel so needy," Christiane said. "I feel so pushed away and not seen and not appreciated."

"But if you do things to be unkind to him and stick him, of course, he is going to continue pushing you away," Ariel said.

"You have consistently done things to get him to reject you so you could be right," Shya said. "Do you see that?"

"Yes, I see that," Christiane admitted.

The desire to be right is deeply ingrained in most of us, sometimes so much so that we choose it over having a satisfying and fulfilling life. But you cannot have both at the same time. Either you're being right or you're experiencing well-being. For example, if you're in a traffic jam and someone cuts in front of you, either you shrug it off or you sit and fume. If you choose the former, then you choose your own well-being. If you choose the latter, you choose to suffer. When you up the stakes from traffic jams to rejecting a parent so you can feel rejected, then you increase the level of your suffering.

Many people are attached to being right and they argue for their right to be upset. They stamp their feet and say, "But they did something wrong, so they deserve to be punished."

But however justified you may feel in being right and holding a grudge, you're choosing to suffer. If you let it go, you're choosing to be alive.

Before this conversation, Christiane had not seen how her resistance to her father's point of view actually perpetuated the fight. Have you ever heard the saying, "The apple doesn't fall far from the tree?" It's entirely possible that her father felt "needy, unseen and pushed away" also. Maybe his anti-Semitic remarks were his way to get Christiane's attention. Father and daughter had been locked in this dynamic of conflict for a long time, and her compassion was the key to resolving it. Letting go of her grudge didn't mean she was endorsing his views. It meant that she was willing to stop the fight from her side.

A healthy relationship is never a 50-50 deal. If you want to have a Match Made in Heaven, you must take 100% responsibility for your relationship and the health of it. That's why we say, "It takes two to fight and one to end the fight—and that one always has to be you."

When Shya pointed out to Christiane what she'd been doing, she suddenly saw the truth. In that moment, something settled within her. In an instant, the fight with her father dropped away and Christiane looked tired and relieved as if a long struggle was finally over.

"I see this," she said again.

"Okay, Christiane. Now don't judge yourself for having done it. This fight was the idea of a two-year-old that you never brought awareness to before. Now that you see it, you don't have to do it any more if you don't want to."

"I look at my parents now and I realize that it's not about me needing anything from them, Christiane," Ariel said. "My attitude as the adult woman that I am is looking for what I have to give. You're never going to be able to feed that two-year-old enough attention for her to be happy—but you're not two anymore."

"Congratulations," Shya said with a laugh, "there is a possibility of having a life now, *your* life, not in opposition to anything. Your life up to now has been defined by being in opposition to your father. You don't have to do that anymore."

"Here's a hint," Ariel said. "If I were you, I'd operate as if those times when you're feeling needy are times when you've just stopped expressing yourself."

Christiane looked thoughtful. "Yes," she said, nodding.

"When you really express yourself, you get excited. For example, I know you sell some lovely cleaning products. When you get excited about that, you're no longer needy. When you do feel needy, that's just a clue that you've stopped going for your life and started looking to get something, as if 'they' should be giving it to you."

"Wow, that's right. Every time I'm needy, I am really…" she paused, momentarily at a loss for words. "I piss people off because I'm so stubborn. My attitude is like, 'Come on, give me something.' And they…"

She paused again. Perhaps she was seeing a string of pictures, little movies replaying the times she had been needy and demanding. She certainly had just described the dynamic that she had repeatedly played out, not only with her father but with her husband as well. Christiane would get upset, re-enact the temper tantrum set in place by a two-year-old, and then she would demand attention in a highly unattractive, uninviting manner. This behavior generated the opposite of what she really wanted, but it was true to her agenda to prove that her father was unkind. Determined to prove that her father rejected her and that he was a bad person, she was bound to create and recreate events that bore out that perspective.

"When you're like that, people push that needy, demanding version of you away," Shya finished for her. "You don't like needy people, do you?"

Christiane stared at him dumbly.

"Do you?" he said.

Still no response.

"Do you like being around needy people, Christiane?" he asked again.

Still she stared. It was as if her internal circuits were fried. If she answered, "No, I don't like needy people," then she might have to take responsibility for all the times the men in her life seemed to reject her.

"Is your English not working very well right now?" Shya joked, eliciting a laugh.

"I'm thinking," she said, trying to buy time as she formulated a response.

"She just doesn't want to answer," Ariel pointed out.

"True. She doesn't want to answer that question," Shya replied.

"What should I say?" Christiane finally said. "No.

I have the impression I am not around needy people that much."

"But, truthfully, you don't like to be around them either. If you want people to enjoy being around you, be who you are, not the story about how you're a needy person. You're not needy at all. You're so strong." Shya said.

"And self-sufficient," Ariel added.

"And self-sufficient," Shya repeated. "You just pretend to be needy."

Christiane started to laugh, really laugh. She saw the truth. She really was strong and self-sufficient. "Needy" was just the symptom of a temper tantrum that had been turned into a lifestyle. Seeing the truth without judgment lightened the burden her childhood story had placed on her heart.

"Guess what, Christiane," Ariel said. "If you aren't needy, but you think you are, no matter what somebody gives you or does for you, no matter how much attention they give you, it's not going to fulfill that need because you're not actually needy. It's just a thought. It's not reality."

"Thank you," Christiane said.

Her thanks had depth and meaning. Her true elegance had come back to the foreground, as the petulant child had been seen, not judged and had disappeared in an instant.

"You're welcome," Shya replied. "And thank *you*."

Compassion Begins at Home
TransformationMadeEasy.com/matchmadeinheaven

14

BEHAVIORS AND BELIEFS

As we grow up, we learn ways to think and act that become our pre-programmed behaviors and beliefs, which we bring into adulthood. For example, perhaps you learned to express your anger passively, with a roll of your eyes or in the tone of your voice. Or perhaps you learned that fighting was a form of foreplay and essential to an exciting relationship. If you grew up in Japan, you probably favored fish and rice for dinner. If you were raised in Italy, more likely than not you preferred pasta, automatically assuming that this was the way food should be prepared. These are just a few examples of the millions of behaviors and beliefs you absorbed as a child, which quickly became so ingrained that you accepted them without question or qualification.

As children, from the time of our birth until the age of six, we exist in a mental state comparable to being hypnotized. Our young brains run on theta brainwaves, meaning we accept everything we see and hear around us as the unequivocal Truth. Everything we learn from our parents, our families and our society at large is assimilated and automatically assumed to be true or accurate.

We have no control over this. We simply absorb all the information and draw upon it every day for the rest of our lives.

One might think that Christiane rejected her father's culture at age two, but in reality this was not the case. What she railed against was the attention that her father gave to her brother and not to her. She didn't reject the culture—she simply wanted his attention, and fighting him was the childish strategy that she employed.

Our early socialization becomes our blueprint for how we live and relate, so if we never take an objective look at our behaviors and beliefs, we'll never think or act any differently. We'll continue to roll our eyes or have fiery, painful relationships or, as we will see in the following conversation with Joe, enjoy eating pasta that is cooked a certain way. We'll wonder why we have problems and why we cannot seem to control our impulses, even when they're clearly destructive. Until we start to recognize these behaviors and beliefs for what they are without judging them, they will have complete control over our lives.

Over the years, we have worked with thousands of people, all of whom grew up with beliefs and behaviors they carried unquestioningly into later life. Since folks initially have no control over their reactions, we have come to refer to these ways of relating as "mechanical behaviors." As people become familiar with our anthropological, transformational approach, they begin to notice the way they respond or react to life without judging themselves for what they discover. This allows habituated, mechanical behaviors to dissolve in the light of awareness.

Self-observation without self-reproach is a deeply liber-
ating experience that enables people, often for the first
time in their lives, to discover what is *really* true for
them, not what they've always believed to be The Truth.

DISCOVERING YOUR TRUTH

In this section we meet Joe, a good-looking man in his
early 30s, of Italian-American descent, with short black
hair and wide dark-rimmed glasses. He explained that
since his relationship of 18 months had recently ended,
he felt ready to start dating again.

"I'm single now," Joe said. "I'm excited to date and I'm
excited about new possibilities. But at the same time, I
also have a feeling that it might be too soon and I may be
trying to override certain emotions."

"Do you believe that you need to have a mourning
period because your relationship ended?" Ariel asked
lightly with a smile.

"Yes," Joe admitted, laughing a little.

"Because," Shya said, "you're afraid of being seen as a
womanizer."

"Yes," Joe laughed again, a little surprised and embarrassed that he held this belief. But it was clear that this
sentiment had not originated from Joe. It was the result
of attitudes he'd learned as a child. Joe didn't realize that
this was something he had absorbed, along with the food
he ate and the air he breathed. Now, as an adult, it was
not how he really felt. It was how he thought he *should*
feel. And this judgment, unbeknownst to Joe, was keeping him from having a fulfilling dating life.

"Okay, so here's the thing," Shya said. "You're already
married."

Joe's brow furrowed and he looked confused. "How so?" he asked slowly.

"Well," Shya asked, "who might you be married to?"

Joe began thinking, searching for the answer. Still rather unsure, he ventured a guess. "My ex-girlfriend?"

"No," we both said.

Then the answer dawned and Joe gave a sheepish smile. "My mother," he said.

"Exactly," Shya said. "And what is your mother's opinion of men who date many women?"

At this, Joe started to look a little uncomfortable and uncertain. He rolled his head back and contemplated. "Not a good one," he said.

"If you started dating now," Ariel said, "dating multiple people in a week, just to try them on for size, and your mom found out, what would she think?"

He said, "She'd think I was getting around."

"Is that a good thing," Shya asked, "or a bad thing?"

Joe brought his finger up to his chin, pondering. "A bad thing," he said finally.

"Because it's not what she raised you to be," Shya clarified. "She raised you to be a one-woman man."

"Yes," his voice faltered slightly as he responded.

"Do you notice," Shya observed, "how you're hesitating, sorting through what I'm saying in your mind? You're not simply being here. You're defending your mother in your thoughts because you think I'm somehow impugning her character. But I'm an anthropologist looking at how you're relating to your life. You have a very strong connection in relationship to your mom and you want her approval."

"Yes," Joe admitted, though he was obviously still a little uncomfortable with the topic of conversation and the direction he thought it was taking. "Yes," he repeated.

"We're not suggesting you sever your relationship with

your mom," Ariel added. "We're talking about compensating for the currents in your life."

When people have a very close relationship with one or both of their parents, one where they are very attached to the beliefs and behaviors in which they were raised, and when they still strongly identify with their culture of origin, they can be reluctant to acknowledge that some of these ways of thinking and acting might not always be beneficial. But when they're able to look at their parents, family and culture objectively, then they can start to see what works for them and what doesn't.

COMPENSATING FOR THE CURRENTS IN YOUR ENVIRONMENT

Looking at the way your culture has shaped your thoughts and behaviors does not mean you have to reject it in order to learn your own truth and make your own choices. If you did so, you wouldn't be any closer to knowing the real you. Reacting in opposition to your upbringing, doing the opposite of everything you learned growing up, has the same result as accepting it all without question. In both cases you are still defining yourself in relation to your upbringing. You still don't know yourself.

We suggested to Joe that he become aware of the beliefs and behaviors that had become ingrained in him. Rather than judging them as right or wrong, we encouraged him to see them like currents. His cultural upbringing was neither good nor bad but was simply there rather like the flow of a river. Once he was aware of the current, he had a choice whether to follow the dictates of the cultural current or not.

"Shya and I have a boat that we use on the river," Ariel explained. "When we've finished using it for the day and Shya drives the boat back up onto the trailer, he has to compensate for the current. If he tries to drive straight up onto the trailer and the current is pushing from left to right, by the time he gets to the trailer, the boat has moved downstream. He has to compensate for the current. Either that, or wait for the river to stop flowing."

Joe gave a little laugh, seeing the impossibility of waiting for the water to stop running before pulling one's boat from the river.

"That's like you and your mom," Ariel continued. "There's a current between you. It's a lovely current. We're not suggesting that you sever things with her. You just need to discover how to compensate for the pressure within yourself to conform to what you believe she wants. In your past relationship with your ex-girlfriend, your mom came between the two of you. You were deferring to how your mom thought about things. Even in the privacy of your own home, when your mother was not there, you thought about what your mom would think and whether or not she would approve of what you were doing."

This is a perfect example of how Joe was being influenced by his upbringing without realizing it. Even in his own home with his then-girlfriend, he was carrying the past into his present life. He was imagining (perhaps completely erroneously) how his mom might feel about certain things and adapting his behavior and opinions accordingly. He was viewing everything through the tinted spectacles of what he believed his mother's attitudes and opinions to be. As a result, he was unable at that time to have a relationship that would be truly satisfying.

"Most people define their lives in relation to whether or not their parents would approve or disapprove of their choices," Shya said. "Some people go for approval, others for disapproval. But they're not looking at what is really true for them. Their lives are defined by either being or not being like their parents. If you want to have a relationship, Joe, you're going to have to separate yourself so you can find out what is true for you in relationship to a woman. This is better than doing things on the sly so your mother doesn't find out."

As we talked, a new perspective was beginning to open for Joe. "Yes, I see that."

"When I said you're already married," Shya explained, "I meant it's going to be very difficult for you to have a new relationship when your primary relationship is still with your mom. This is not to malign your mom in any way. I believe she's a very nice lady. But she lives her life mechanically through what she believes to be true and correct. She doesn't stop to look at what her truth is. She just behaves in ways dictated by her cultural upbringing."

"Yes," Joe agreed, "I know my family and I have a strong cultural upbringing that dictates my behavior."

"Whether it's appropriate or not," Shya added.

"Exactly," Joe confirmed. Gradually, he was starting to see just how many of his beliefs and behaviors were not actually his, but had been passed on to him by his culture, bequeathed by the hundreds of thousands of relatives that had come before him.

But Joe still wasn't seeing his family, especially his mother, through an adult perspective. He was seeing her as he had when he was a small child. During those early years, when his reality was limited and extremely subjective, he developed an impression of his mom and her beliefs, including the belief that she wouldn't approve of her son dating multiple women. But it was likely that he hadn't actually given much thought to his mother's current values. He certainly hadn't directly asked her for her opinion to ascertain how she really felt.

It's true that, just like us, our parents hold limiting beliefs about things that they imbibed from their culture without question or qualification. It's also equally possible that we assume they believe something that they actually don't. It's entirely likely that, having put together a picture of them when you were very young, you haven't stopped to notice how they really feel and think today. When this is the case, you will continue to seek the approval (or disapproval), not of your parents, but of your *idea* of who your parents are.

Sometimes we meet individuals whose parents died many years before. These people are often still gearing their lives in agreement with or opposition to the phantom of their mom or dad. But when awareness is brought to this habit, a person can live his or her life unfettered from that constraint.

THE POWER OF THE PAST
ON THE PRESENT

Social/cultural/familial influences can continue to have a powerful effect on your present day life. When they do, you will react without thinking and find yourself speaking and acting in ways that are at times inappropriate to your present environment. To highlight this, Ariel offered Joe a humorous example from his own life so it would be easy for him to see it without judgment.

"I heard from your last girlfriend," Ariel said, "that there came a time when she made the 'grievous error' of putting red sauce over broccoli and actually enjoying it. But she said you were appalled because that's not how Italians do it."

Joe burst out laughing. "It was automatic," he admitted. "I just saw the red sauce that she had put together with broccoli and I reacted."

"It's not just your mom who has been enculturated. You have been, too," Ariel explained. "Now it's time for you to start investigating what you hold to be true. Otherwise you can get disgusted over the idea of red sauce on broccoli."

We all laughed at this funny example. In the levity of the moment, Joe was able to see his cultural upbringing and how deeply his behaviors and beliefs were ingrained in him. In this small, seemingly silly example, he could see how he'd been viewing his world through a cultural lens. Now that he knew about it, he could start to compensate for that particular prescription and begin to see the world anew. Joe was now free to discover his own unique perspective—one that wasn't dictated by, nor in opposition to the culture he grew up in—a perspective that wasn't based on his desire to get his mother's approval, either.

"People have body sensations and they believe them to be the truth," Shya said, referring to the automatic disgust that Joe had experienced when he saw red sauce on broccoli. "Well, maybe they're not the truth. Your gut feeling may not be accurate. It may just be your programming. Isn't that exciting?"

"Yes, it is," Joe agreed, his eyes lighting up.

"When we're out on our boat on the ocean and the fog rolls in," said Shya, "I have no visual reference for where I'm heading. Even if I want to go straight ahead, I always seem to steer the boat to the left. It's amazing. I swear I'm going straight, but the boat always veers to the left. I know that through the GPS and radar systems."

Joe listened, eager to follow Shya's analogy.

"You have to trust your instruments," Shya explained, "not your impulses. In your case, you need to pay attention to how the people around you respond to things you say and do, because on occasion, your point of view is askew."

"You do that by looking, by being there," Ariel explained. "For example, if you blurt out, 'Pasta sauce over broccoli? That's not Italian!' and if you're there to see your girlfriend's reaction, you'll know in that instant that

you've said something mechanical and potentially hurtful. Saying, 'I'm sorry,' goes a long way at that point.
When you behave in a knee-jerk way that isn't nice, and
if you see it without judging it or defending yourself for
having done it, you can usually clean up the mess by
apologizing."

"You've been taught how to be a man in the culture
where you grew up," Shya explained. "The way you relate to women is predetermined by that culture. Not by
you, Joe the human being, but by Joe the Italian man
who has machismo or a role to play that has been predetermined by the culture itself. Do you see that?"

"Yes," Joe nodded. He was no longer pausing to consider things. He could clearly see the truth of how his
culture had influenced his behaviors. "Yes, absolutely."

TRANSFORMING YOUR ABILITY TO RELATE

Recognizing the ways your behavior and beliefs have
been preconditioned by your culture is key to having a
Match Made in Heaven. Until you begin to notice the
familial and cultural beliefs and behaviors that you have
adopted, you will continue to live through them and
view the world in a way that will be reactionary, a recreation of the past. For example, Joe believed that his mom
disapproved of his dating multiple women, so he had a
challenge when faced with the whole dating process. In
reality, dating more than one gal was not only healthy,
but necessary.

Nowadays many people use the Internet as a tool when
looking for dates. There are many dating websites, such
as Match.com and eHarmony, where it is reasonable and
expected for a man (or a woman, for that matter) to start
a dialogue with several perspective dates with an aim of
eventually meeting those that seem promising. Oftentimes folks will talk by phone and then perhaps meet for

a coffee just to test out if there is any chemistry in person. Imagine how odd it would be if Joe went online and picked out one lady by reading her profile, and tried to turn her into his girlfriend before he met her to see what she was like in person.

In this day and age, while using a dating website as a tool, the "one-man-for-one-woman" theory certainly doesn't work, particularly at the beginning of the process. In today's world, Joe doesn't live in a small village where dating the only three eligible girls in his age range, who all know each other, would be potentially upsetting in that tiny community. The old ideas that may have originated in a time frame where there was a stigma attached to dating without a chaperone going along to make sure that the parties all behave, no longer apply. Rules that are a vestige of an antiquated system may still be part of the way you were raised, but they may not be appropriate for today's complexities.

"In order to have a relationship that will work," Shya explained, "you have to disengage from your cultural upbringing and start to discover what it feels like to be with this woman or that woman rather than assuming you already know how to be. You have an idea, pre-determined by your culture, of how you are supposed to behave in a relationship. Now, to have a really successful relationship you will have to surrender to the moment rather than blindly follow an idea of where it's going. You have to slow things down and get here."

"Okay," Joe nodded.

"I like that you said that," Shya replied. "Because at the beginning of this conversation, you were sorting through what I was saying rather than just hearing what I was saying. Now your answers are crisper, more direct, more here in this moment. Transformation has happened, now that you are here. Transformation happens when you get here into this moment of your life, not when you are thinking about what is being said. And it feels very different."

"Yes," Joe agreed, his eyes shining brightly, "yes it does!"

"This moment is very alive," Shya said. "But in your head, it is very protected and measured, as though there is a maze in your mind that the conversation has to get through to reach you. And that is not being alive, it's being careful. It's surviving. It's safe but very unsatisfying."

We could see the transformation in Joe's face, how bright and suddenly three-dimensional he appeared. During the course of the conversation, he had seen his mechanical behaviors and gradually allowed himself to listen to us without filtering our words, without resisting them or agreeing with them. He simply listened to hear what was said from our point of view. He'd stepped into the present moment and was feeling truly alive. From this perspective, the possibility of a Match Made in Heaven became available.

When Joe started to see the ways he had been programmed by his culture, and how he had been holding onto his mother's opinions, whether real or imagined, he was able to really *be* with us. Now he could really *be* with his dates also rather than, metaphorically speaking, have his mother come between them.

"We are excited for you," Ariel said.

"Yes," Joe grinned. "Me too."

Discovering Your Truth
TransformationMadeEasy.com/matchmadeinheaven

15

APPROVAL AND DISAPPROVAL: FLIP SIDES OF THE SAME COIN

*E*arlier, we saw how Christiane's fight with her father twisted her way of relating. Her actions weren't independent and she wasn't living her own life. Since she could only comfortably do those things that opposed her father and his values, a large part of her energy and life "choices" were skewed in relation to resisting him, his beliefs and the culture he represented. When naming her children, for instance, she did not have the option to consider all the names that she liked. Her pool of potential names was narrowly defined, predetermined to be only those that would be obviously "Jewish" and therefore disturbing to her father. Christiane's life and life strategy was about going for his disapproval. It got her lots of negative attention and it became an integral part of her identity.

That is one of the most common types of incompletion with one's parents—where you don't live *your* life. Instead, you live "not *their* life." In other words, your actions are predetermined in resistance and opposition to someone, like your father or mother, along with their church, beliefs, values or ideologies. In effect, you look to see what they would do or prefer and then you do the opposite.

Another common type of incompletion with one's parents is perhaps a bit more subtle in its control over your life, but it can just as strongly predetermine your actions. This is when you structure your life in compliance with the cultural beliefs and rules in which you were raised and you live your life in order to garner your parents' approval. This also extends to the community in which you were raised. When this is the case, you are not looking at what is true for you. Rather, your actions are twisted by your need to insure someone else's approval.

Take Joe for example. When he absorbed the values of his culture and his mother, his mind was young, unformed and could not actually grasp the complexities of being an adult who dates and relates to others. Joe's strong family, with both a mother and a father in residence, set in place for him the concept that a "good" man had only one woman—his wife. But Joe did not know his mother and father when they were dating, so he wasn't privy to the ups and downs on their road to finding one another and ultimately marrying. Joe also came to adulthood at a time when dating was more complex than in his parents' day.

His parents had been born and raised in a neighborhood that was filled with Americans of Italian descent. Today, Joe, still living in Brooklyn, lives and works in a multi-ethnic, multi-cultural stew. He has friends of different religions, races, genders, sexual orientation, nationalities and ages. One of Joe's good friends is in his 70s, while others are in their mid-20s, and many fall in between. When the ideas of good and bad, right and wrong were put in place for Joe, he could not have conceived of such an expanded pool of friends, much less online dating, texting and emails.

Joe's mother has now evolved from the person she was when Joe was in his formative years. After he had grown up and moved away from home, she started a successful business of her own—a small gourmet cafe in Manhattan's financial district. We expect that her pool of friends, acquaintances and her ideas about life have grown as well, but when you're young and you absorb ideas, they become a background filter through which you view life. The truth is that Joe wasn't actually locked into the unaware mechanical behavior of trying to get his mother's approval. Instead, he was unwittingly trying to get the approval of a fantasy version of his mom. In other words, his childhood impressions of who his mother was and what she liked and disliked were superimposed on his life—a set of ideas that may or may not have been based in reality.

In actuality, Joe's mother may not have had a problem with his going out with several ladies in order to find a woman with whom he shares a true connection and can build a life. It is entirely possible that Joe registered his mother's desire to see him happy, find a mate and build a family. Then he ran it through his internalized ideas of a "good" man. His concept of what is a good man or what is a bad man could have been based on something he overheard as a three- or four-year-old. Forgotten incidents unknowingly can predetermine an adult's behaviors and choices. Things that you have overheard, unspoken attitudes that you have witnessed and the body language of those around you can form prejudices such as the one Joe had been holding against men who played the field.

Joe's relationship with his ex-girlfriend had been stressed by his unexamined attachments to his mother and the Italian-American culture in which he was raised. Those attachments acted as a barrier between him and the gal he was dating. Many times people develop attachments to someone or something as a buffer between themselves and the world.

When Shya was a young man, he had a first-hand experience of just how this dynamic works and how pining for a fantasy "someone" can keep you from seeing the people directly in front of you. In the next chapter, written from Shya's point of view, you will see how his brief encounter with a young woman from Detroit had a profound effect on his ability to be present and available.

16

DETROIT SHARON

$\mathcal{A}$s I look back some 50-odd years ago, I am amazed by how fresh the events are in my memory. I was 21 years old and I was scheduled to leave home in three weeks to begin a semester of courses at the University of Hawaii. At that time I was living in New York City and completing my classes at New York University when my next-door neighbor, Wendy, had a girlfriend visit from their hometown of Detroit. Her name was Sharon and she was very, very cute with short dark hair, large eyes, and a petite, sexy body. We were immediately attracted to each other.

When Sharon and I began flirting, we quickly discovered that I was leaving in three weeks for Hawaii and soon she was going back to Detroit. It added a sense of urgency to the situation. There was no possibility of a long-term relationship. There was just a hot, passionate fling. It lasted for about a week and then she went home. Shortly thereafter, I ended up in Hawaii. Ostensibly, I was taking some classes, but in actuality, I was primarily surfing the classic breaks on the south shore and the north shore of the island. I really can't remember anything about the courses I took at the University, but I do remember following my passion for surfing. I stayed on Oahu for eight months.

At first I lived in Waikiki, but for the majority of my stay I lived on Kainui Road with a pack of young surfers. In the morning, afternoon or evening, whenever the surf was up, we would step out our door, grab our boards and head down to the beach to the Bonsai Pipeline.

December came and the weather grew stormy thousands of miles away at sea, which produced huge swells and prodigious surf. On Christmas day, we all piled into a Volkswagen van and went to Waimea Bay. We stood for hours, watching the giant waves crest and crash on the shore. Finally three surfers, two experts and a fool, paddled out to attempt to ride the 30-foot walls of water. The experts were a couple of guys who had braved the elements and surfed the big ones for years. The fool was a lanky 21-year-old, me.

I managed to stay on my board and I didn't die, I'm happy to say. At the end of the day there were plenty of people to pat me on the back and loads of girls in bikinis who where suitably impressed. You see, one of the side benefits of surfing, aside from the exercise, was the girls. It was amazing how many beautiful girls were in Hawaii. There was only one problem. I was "in love" with Detroit Sharon and I wrote to her almost every day. In truth, I was a shy young man, afraid of dating and somewhat socially inept. Having a long distance relationship was a very convenient way of avoiding my shy nature when relating to girls. I was in a relationship, at least in my mind. And I thought that going out with other women would be a betrayal.

Of course, I had a few dates while I was on the North Shore. Out of the many opportunities presenting themselves to me, I didn't avoid them all. But as I recall, if I went out for a beer with a girl, there would be three of us actually sitting at the table—me, my date and the ghost of Sharon. I was not fully with whomever I was relating to. Somewhere in the back of my mind, I was comparing the girl I was talking with to the growing list of attributes I had assigned to Sharon in my ever-expanding fantasy about who she was and what she meant to me.

This long distance relationship served many purposes. I could consider myself in a relationship, so I never actually had to confront my fear of dating and the possibility of being rejected. The fantasy of Sharon sustained me in my aloneness. I siphoned off the intensity of the moment with dreams of our time together from the past, which were now re-scripted to be larger than life, while constructing a happily-ever-after scenario for the future. One would think that as a surfer I was interested in experiencing the intensity of life. Perhaps so, but interpersonally, I was inept and insecure. During those eight months, even though I was young and single and relatively available, I had very few dates. They never really amounted to anything, since my heart was attached to my fantasy of my relationship with Detroit Sharon.

As the time grew closer to leave Hawaii, I arranged my flight home via Detroit. But the long anticipated reunion was actually a rude awakening. The shocking truth was that it took me all of one day to realize the mistake I had made. Sharon was still cute but we had nothing in common. It didn't take long to see that I didn't even really like her. Suddenly I realized that the person I had fantasized about was just that, a fantasy. This person only looked like the Sharon of my dreams. The two of us limped through the rest of our visit and we were both relieved when I left. Sharon eventually went on to become a lawyer and a judge and I went on to New York and the rest of my life.

Nowadays, when people talk with us about their long distance relationships, I am reminded of those eight months I spent in Hawaii rejecting many beautiful women for the fantasy of my "relationship." When I was in Hawaii, I thought that something in the future, namely Sharon, was going to save me. Once I made it back to New York, I complained to myself about the mistake I had made to avoid all of those beautiful bikini-clad girls. My life at that time was a pendulum swing between the past and future and Detroit Sharon had been a very convenient shield between me and living my life.

It is easy to be seduced by the dream of a better "some day" or the fantasy of how the past was so fine. These flights of fancy are convenient side trips, when faced with something new or challenging that has yet to be mastered. From time to time I chuckle when I think of Detroit Sharon and the lesson I learned about not throwing away this moment for some fictitious someday that will, in fact, never come.

17

BEING "RIGHT" VS.
BEING "ALIVE"

*I*n most relationships, an ongoing fight simmers just
below the surface. Sometimes the conflict appears subtle
but at other times it is outright war. People have grown
up in a sea of discord and have been socialized to expect
it and accept it. In other words, fighting is "normal." In
the next section we will meet 3 individuals:
* Nisha, whose relationship is fairly new
* Charlotte, who has been married for
  more than 50 years
* Caitlin, whose marriage is still in its youth
With varying degrees of success, these ladies are seeing
that their need to be right has led to pain and discord in
their respective relationships.

Transformation is both instantaneous and cumulative.
In a moment, you can see an old mechanical way of relating to your mate. If you don't judge this behavior, it
can have a profound impact on your ability to live in
harmony. With practice, you get better at letting go of
the need to have your perspective be the right one.

YOU'RE WRONG! I'M RIGHT!

When it comes to creating a Match Made in Heaven, giving up being right is one of the essential ingredients.

Let's take a moment to define what we mean by "being right." It's when you take on an adversarial relationship to someone, making them wrong and yourself right. When you take this position, nothing they say or do will convince you to give up your point of view. After all, holding onto your point of view is the prime directive. You will rehearse and rehash your position in your thoughts, because proving the other person wrong becomes your life's mission. When locked in a right/wrong battle, there can be no surrender, no relaxation. It's a battle that you have to win and they have to lose.

Very few of us have had role models who were skilled enough at letting go of the point they wanted to make to truly listen to their partner. We have been trained to think that if you set down the fight, you're losing something. Living in a win/lose dynamic is one of the hallmarks of a change modality. Remember that most people are trying to change their relationship and are picking on themselves and each other. When you take a transformational approach to dating, relating and marriage, you'll find that the dynamic becomes win/win.

Most of us have been trained to expect that there is a right one and a wrong one. When this is the case, the relationship is a constant struggle. The participants have daily skirmishes in the ongoing war, constantly trying to be the one who scores the most points, the one who comes out on top. When this is the case, we conscript troops—our friends—to take our side in the ongoing conflict as we complain and gather agreement that we are right and that our partner is wrong.

When you're locked in this type of battle, there can be no true partnership. If you're holding onto your own point of view, refusing to see your partner's point of view, there will always be tension between the two of you, limiting the level of intimacy and love that you're able to experience together. It's as if you're in a continuous not-so-friendly game of tug-of-war, pulling on the relationship rope with your partner pulling on the opposing side. When you're habituated to being right, there is no harmony between you and your mate. A conflict of wills is always brewing just below the surface, waiting to burst into flame much like a glowing ember which is covered with a deceptive coating of soft grey ash.

BEING ALIVE

Our definition of aliveness is to have love, health, happiness, full self-expression, relationship and partnership. To feel close with your partner, to feel loving and in relationship, you need to set down your overwhelming need to be right because you can't have both intimacy and being right at the same time. If you let go of being right, then you can have a Match Made in Heaven.

However, when you are tenaciously holding onto your perspective that your point of view is correct and your partner's is wrong, in that moment you destroy the heavenly nature of your union. You can think of this like a light switch, a toggle switch. It's either on or it's off. There is no rheostat. Nowadays there are rheostats on many lights so you can turn them on just a little bit. Not so with being right. You can't be just a little right.

We understand that letting go of the idea that you're right and the other is wrong can be very challenging at first. It's hard to let go of generations of conditioning. Many people are afraid that if they let go of the war, they'll lose themselves and become a doormat. Here is a classic example of just such a fight.

THE POPEYE FACTOR

When we sat down with Nisha, she had only known us for a few short weeks. It was enough time for her to get an inkling that there was another possibility, but the fight in her, the need to be right, was still firmly in control. It reminded us of Popeye in the old cartoons when he was fighting Bluto. In the Popeye cartoons, when it came to a fight, there would be a big cloud of dust surrounding the altercation and from time to time Popeye would pop his head out of the dust cloud to comment and laugh about the fight before returning to the fray. Here is what happened during our conversation with Nisha.

Nisha is a pretty young woman of Indian decent with glossy black, shoulder-length hair. She was wearing a magenta-colored sweater and a white scarf. She sat down with us and laid out her problem.

"I have something I want to ask you about what happened this morning between my boyfriend and me. It was something that I've always done, but this time I noticed it. It felt like I stepped out of myself for a moment, saw myself doing something and then went right back into it and continued doing it. I was struggling with myself, thinking, *stop it*, but I just kept going back and forth. I was upset about a very a simple thing: He didn't do the dishes!"

Nisha laughed at herself and seemed almost embarrassed by the petty nature of the conflict. Yet it was easy to see that she felt she was in the right and he was in the wrong.

"When I woke up this morning, the dishes were still in the sink," she said. "They had been there the night before and my boyfriend was supposed to wash them. Because I did the cooking, I said, 'You have to do the dishes because I don't like doing them!'"

We could see the fight in Nisha. For a moment,

she stepped out of the dust cloud of her conflict and laughed, but in the next moment her reality (that she was right and he was wrong and should have done the dishes) snapped right back into place.

It was clear by the tension in her body and the tightness in her expression that Nisha was still in the midst of the fight, both with herself and her boyfriend. Quite new to transformation but touched by its magic, Nisha had become aware of two possibilities: to get angry and feel self-righteous about it, or to let go of her anger and feel well in herself and in partnership with her boyfriend. She struggled with these two realities, going back and forth but ultimately, as she was sitting there with us that morning, the anger had won the fight, at least for the moment.

BEING RESPONSIBLE FOR THE HEALTH OF YOUR RELATIONSHIP

Nisha's fight is common to many couples who haven't yet learned the nature of true partnership. In fact, we bet that many of you reading this chapter have already picked a side. You may be commenting, "Yeah, he should do his share." Others may be thinking, "She's just like my girlfriend—always nagging on me."

Sharing a new possibility, Shya gave Nisha some examples from our partnership.

"Ariel and I are experts in the area of relationship. We've been together for 28 years, married 26 of those, and we're still passionate. In our reality, each of us does whatever needs to be done. It's not as though I'm doing Ariel's job if I wash the dishes. It's not as if I'm doing Ariel's job if I cook dinner. It's not as if I'm doing her job if I do both or either of those things. Ariel likes to wash the clothes and I don't have much skill with that. But I like to iron the clothes and I'm very good at that. The job doesn't matter. If you're keeping a list of 'I did my 50%, he should do his 50%,' then the relationship will never work because relationship is 100%/100%. You are 100% responsible for the health of your relationship, from your point of view."

STICKING TO HER STORY

A sudden smile flickered across Nisha's face as she recognized the truth of what Shya said. But just as quickly, it vanished and the desire to be right seized her again. Immediately Nisha returned to her rendition of the unwashed dishes and it was clear that she was still sticking to her story: She was right and her boyfriend was wrong.

"What happened," she said, "was that I got up to make breakfast and then I noticed the dishes in the sink. Some of the dishes I needed to use to make breakfast were still not washed. So then I started huffing and puffing and he was still lying down. It's a studio apartment, so it's not like he couldn't hear me.

"In my mind I was thinking, *I'm just going to wash the coffee pot and the pan and the spatula because that's what I need right now.* And then I said to myself, *I could just wash them all.* Then I thought, *No, he has to wash them! Why didn't he wash them last night?*

"So then, I'm cooking and I'm hearing myself. Everything's falling from my hands now because I'm agitated, irritated, frustrated, and I'm trying to get all of this done fast enough to get here this morning."

By now Nisha was on a roll. She brought the conflict with her so completely we could almost see her huffing and puffing and clattering the pots and pans. She sounded so normal.

When we let her know that her reality was typical, she laughed and continued, "He was still lying in bed and said, 'I don't feel like going to the gym this morning.'

And I'm thinking, *Well, at least you could get up and wash the dishes.* I didn't tell that to him, but I'm thinking that."

The dishes had soaked in the sink all night and Nisha had been soaking in resentment all morning, furious and steeped in her own righteousness. As she defended her point of view, it was clear she thought her boyfriend was lazy, lying in bed while she huffed and puffed away in the kitchen, clattering the dirty dishes. In her reality he was thoughtless and annoying. He should have done the dishes but he hadn't. Nothing else mattered to Nisha in that moment.

More than once during the conversation, we asked her if it would have been a very big deal for her to wash those dirty dishes herself. Occasionally another quick smile flitted across her face as she recognized the petty nature of her argument and attachment to being right. But then she would just shrug, her habituation to being right winning out again as she continued to defend her point of view. She wasn't really looking at how to dissolve the fight—especially if it meant that she should take responsibility for the fact that he hadn't done the dishes on the previous evening. She didn't want to look at the possibility that the way she spoke to him actually kept him from doing those dishes. She batted our suggestions back like tennis balls, rejecting the possibility of transformation, denying herself the chance to create her own Match Made in Heaven.

Nisha's fighting nature was strong. When her boyfriend didn't do what she wanted, she spoke to him with attitude, both aloud and in her thoughts, punishing him for not doing what she thought he should do. Although part of her wanted his love, wanted them both to be happy and to feel alive and well, a still greater part wanted to be right. It didn't matter how miserable it made her, it didn't matter that it might destroy her relationship, she just couldn't let it go.

We continued to offer Nisha the possibility of transforming her attitude and her relationship. We said she could drop the fight whenever she wanted to, and rediscover her aliveness. We shared details of the relationship we have created and the communication style that works so well for us.

Ariel explained, "I can have Shya do anything. He can have me do anything. We are very responsive to each other. But it doesn't happen by beating each other to get what we want. You've learned that being nasty or unkind is a style of communication that is acceptable. But it is absolutely unacceptable in our home. Neither one of us speaks to each other with attitude, not even in our minds. We don't stomp around thinking, "Why don't you do...?"

Listening without interrupting, Nisha was clearly curious. But the expression on her face remained rigid. She was obviously still attached to her right to treat her boyfriend with attitude if she felt he deserved it. She said again, "I *told* my boyfriend to do the dishes, and so he *should* have done them."

There is a difference between a respectful request and a demand made with attitude. A demand of that nature almost ensures that your partner won't comply. No one likes to be told what to do in that way. Even the most willing of partners is going to find it hard to step up and help if you're communicating in a less than respectful manner. It also doesn't work to communicate by banging the pots and pans in order to get attention and express displeasure. Nisha's clattering around that morning expressed her resistance and, as you know, what you resist, persists and grows stronger.

Don't misunderstand us here. We are not saying that Nisha should just buck up and do everything because the relationship is 100% her responsibility. What we are talking about is that Nisha's actions and attitudes made it very difficult to have her relationship be anything other than a fight. "I've done my bit, now you do yours," is not a very attractive attitude, nor a compelling way to make a request. We explained to Nisha that it would be much more effective to share her desires rather than to make demands.

SUCCESSFULLY MAKING A REQUEST

First, it's a good idea to make sure that you have your partner's attention. It does no good to ask something while he or she is preoccupied. Even if your mate is in the room with you, seemingly involved in nothing, he or she could be preoccupied in his or her thoughts. Often one of the two of us will say something such as, "Can I ask you a question?" or "Do you have a moment?"

Once the other says "Yes," a connection is made, we're engaged with each other and it's easy to make a request. This first step is a very important one. If one of us is on the phone and already engaged in a conversation or involved in another activity, and the other simply launches into asking something, the question isn't heard.

Occasionally the answer won't be "Yes." It might be, "I'm in the midst of something. Can you give me five minutes?" Then we speak a few minutes later or renegotiate. Renegotiating the request could be something like, "Can you just answer a quick question?" or "I actually only need a moment if you could give it to me now." And then between the two of us we see the appropriate set of actions to take.

These days, our requests are always respectful. It wasn't always the case for us, but over the years a relaxed climate has been established between the two of us that includes love, compassion and an interest in taking care of each other. It's one thing to say, "Honey, I'm really tired, would you please do the dishes?" It's a very different thing to say, "*Okay*, I've made the dinner, *you* do the dishes."

A smile lit up Nisha's face as she watched us demonstrate communicating with each other, unable to deny the truth of how well it worked and how it created even greater closeness and intimacy between us. We also suggested another possibility. She could simply drop the fight and do the dishes. Indeed, in life she could do things when they presented themselves and not waste precious moments by complaining to herself that she had to do them.

Nisha's smile quickly vanished at that suggestion and her fighting nature rose to the fore again. "No!" she protested. Her boyfriend was *supposed* to do the dishes and he *should* have done them. But just like her boyfriend, Nisha hated being told what to do. Not just in her relationship but everywhere. She didn't like being dominated by the circumstances of her life. If she thought she *had* to do something, she did it begrudgingly and complained to herself that she had to do it. Of course she carried this into her relationship as well. The state of her relationship was simply a reflection of how she related to life.

WIN-WIN

When we cling to our petty natures, it isn't just others who suffer. We also cause pain and stress in ourselves. When you see your petty nature and don't judge yourself for it, it loses its power over your life and your actions reflect this. When you let go of being right, you instantaneously come back into relationship. It was clear that clinging to the fight hadn't created anything but suffering inside Nisha. When she clattered the dishes in her kitchen, silently cursing her boyfriend, she didn't like herself either. She didn't respect herself or her behavior.

Even as she related her experience to us that morning, talking about how wrong her boyfriend was, she was cut off from her love for him. In that moment there was no intimacy.

We continued to demonstrate how she could love and respect herself and create intimacy with her boyfriend. All it took was dropping being right and becoming aware of her mechanical nature and her desire to be right. If she noticed her behavior without judging it, it would dissolve and she would feel loving again. Then her boyfriend would win, she would win, and their relationship could have a chance to become a Match Made in Heaven.

We explained to Nisha that she had a normal relationship, but if she wanted to, she could have an extraordinary one. It was up to her. She could either be right, or her relationship could be magnificent. But she couldn't have both. If Nisha held onto being right, she would punish her boyfriend, stop being intimate and create distance between them. This would not be conducive to creating a true partnership.

At this point having a Match Made in Heaven was not an immediate possibility for Nisha because she didn't want to take 100% responsibility for her relationship. She was still more invested in casting blame and being right that he was wrong.

ENDING THE FIGHT
We told Nisha that it takes two to fight. But it takes only one to end the fight. And it always has to be *you*. We reminded her of our experience of blameless communication, where no one was right or wrong but each just explained his or her needs in that moment. Finally, as the conversation came to an end, we offered Nisha something to take away with her, a picture of two realities: Being Right vs. Being Alive.

Just like Popeye, Nisha had been poking her head out of the clouds of dust, having a chuckle, and then heading straight back in again. She was still determined to be right, but she knew something else was possible. Momentarily, she was already popping out of the fight, the clouds of her own making, and seeing a new possibility. Yet, she kept being swept back into the current of her old reality. But because she was able to step out of the fight, however briefly, we knew she *could* drop it, if she chose. It was entirely up to her and completely within her control. All it would take would be desire on her part, as well as courage and practice.

We don't know if Nisha will ultimately choose a transformational approach to her relationship, if she will triumph over her petty nature and choose partnership and aliveness over the need to be right. But now she has a choice. And that is the magic of transformation.

The Popeye Factor
TransformationMadeEasy.com/matchmadeinheaven

18

100% RESPONSIBILITY

*I*n this chapter we meet Charlotte, a beautiful, elegant woman in her 60s with short grey hair and impeccable makeup, sporting delicate jewelry and a bright blue t-shirt. Charlotte and her husband Bill are two of our oldest and dearest friends. It has been a privilege to share our transformational journey with them since they became friends with Shya in 1963 and were close to us when we were dating and for our entire marriage.

Talented and brilliant in their own right, they are also courageous in their willingness to keep looking at what is possible in their relationship. However, as the following interaction demonstrates, while Charlotte clearly wanted her relationship to fly, she was also reluctant to let go of being right. She was absolutely unwilling to accept responsibility for ending their fight because she wanted it to be a 50-50 deal.

While Charlotte was happy to accept 50% of the "blame," she wanted Bill to take the other 50%. As we will see, this limited her experience of aliveness and intimacy and kept them stuck in petty battles. Throughout the conversation, it was clear that Charlotte really loved Bill and wouldn't consciously want to hurt him or damage their relationship, but it was hard for her to let go of the idea that he was as "guilty" as she was.

Charlotte came to us with questions about a mechanical, repetitive situation but was reluctant to bring it up because it seemed so "silly." We encouraged her to tell us about it because small things can be profoundly impactful on your life and on the health of your relationship.

We likened it to a large bag of dog chow that holds a lot of feed. If you pull on the wrong string, the stitching gets tighter. But if you pull the correct string on the top, it opens completely and the contents are available. In other words, pulling on the correct string unravels the whole bag, or in this case, the entire dynamic.

"When my husband and I have someplace to go," Charlotte said, "and we prepare to leave the house, it gets to the point where one of us is doing something when the other one is ready to go. For instance, Bill will say, 'I'll just finish up.' While he's finishing up, I get involved in something else. Then he's ready, but now he's waiting for me. This goes back and forth and now I'm waiting for him because he started something. It takes a really long time for us to get together and out the door."

UNRAVELING THE DYNAMIC

Our first observation surprised Charlotte. From her account of the situation surrounding leaving their home, we could see that she and Bill, whether they realized it or not, were embroiled in an ongoing fight. Fights can take many different forms and don't need to involve screaming, shouting or throwing things. They can even be conducted in silence. We once had a lady named Valerie at a workshop who insisted that she and her husband never fought. The next day, during the course, she saw a live example of a couple engaged in subtle, silent warfare. "Oh my goodness," she exclaimed, amazed at the realization, "we *do* fight!"

Some people might see Charlotte's situation as an example of just a little "bickering." But bickering is a euphemism for the skirmishes that take place before the war really heats up. If you can catch those little ways that you and your partner pit yourselves against one another and don't judge yourselves, the big blowups won't happen. If you're aware of the flare-ups, you can put out the flame before it becomes a raging inferno.

Charlotte clearly didn't like the suggestion that she and Bill were fighting. Taken aback, she responded with a tentative "Okay," and then laughed along with us as she realized that this wasn't what she had wanted to hear. Her reluctance to recognize the fight came from the fact that she judged it as bad. Instead of seeing it as another mechanical behavior that would dissolve with awareness, Charlotte criticized herself for doing it. In being hard on herself, she was unwilling to take full responsibility for starting and ending the fight. We pointed out to Charlotte that if she didn't judge herself and Bill, she could catch this dynamic and resolve it before it escalated. But only if she just noticed her behavior without judging it.

It is challenging to realize that a relationship is not a 50-50 deal. The health of your relationship is 100% your responsibility from your point of view and 100% your partner's responsibility from his or her point of view. Many people find this difficult because they would prefer to find fault in their partner, collecting good evidence that he or she is the "bad" one, the one in the wrong (as Nisha did in the previous chapter), instead of looking at themselves as the cause and key to ending the fight. Taking 100% responsibility for the state of your relationship can be a humbling experience but also an extremely empowering one. If the fight starts and ends with you, the well-being of your relationship is in your control. It is not decided by the Fates, Cupid or finding the "perfect" partner or your "soul mate." If you're willing to be fully responsible for your relationship, you'll be able to have a Match Made in Heaven.

Charlotte and Bill have been married for 50 years and she loves him deeply. Prior to working with us, they used to fight all the time. In their early years together their relationship was embattled. When they learned about letting go of being right and surrendering to each other, their conflicts greatly reduced in both significance and frequency. But they didn't stop altogether. They still wanted to reserve the right, tucked away in a back pocket, to blame each other.

This was clear when we gave Charlotte's "silly" string another tug. We pointed out how she perpetuated their fight by making him wait in turn after she had been waiting for him. She was getting her revenge, tit-for-tat. Charlotte sat forward and nodded in agreement. But she also reiterated, not for the first time, that the dynamic goes back and forth, demonstrating her attachment to accepting only 50% responsibility. As much as she wanted to end the fight, she also wanted Bill to accept responsibility for his part. She wanted him to be as much in the wrong as she. As long as Charlotte wouldn't release that perspective, as long as she wouldn't take 100% responsibility for starting and ending the fight, they would keep bickering.

LIFE WITHOUT THE FIGHT

We know that Charlotte really wanted to have a Match Made in Heaven and that she was close to it. Ariel gave an example of what life can be like without discord.

"When we're getting ready to leave home, occasionally I'll be ready to go but Shya is completing something. I can either complain about it or find a useful endeavor to occupy my time. I usually put things away or do something in the office or write that extra email. But I have to be prepared to drop it when he's ready to go rather than continuing to work on it as a form of revenge for having been "kept waiting." I happily occupy myself because there's always something in my environment that needs attending to. But in order to do this, you have to be working in concert rather than subtly, or not so subtly, fighting."

Another tug at the silly string revealed a dynamic underlying the fight. Charlotte was temporarily caught in a trap. Unexamined, most people fall prey to a very old mechanical way of relating to life that was set in place in their formative years. We like to call this: Don't Tell Me What To Do.

Two-year-olds have the infantile perspective that doing the opposite of what is requested makes them independent. If we carry this idea into adulthood, Don't Tell Me What To Do can become a life strategy in an individual's tool kit for survival. Resisting your partner's requests or routinely doing the opposite of what is asked will sabotage your well-being rather than protect it. It's a very old, ingrained, mechanical way of relating and it's not uncommon for a person to feel driven to assert their independence when none is needed.

When we reminded Charlotte that it takes one person to end the fight, and it "always has to be you," she nodded quickly, saying, "Right, right," in agreement. But her face was serious and her answer was too quick, falling on top of our words. It was clear that while she agreed intellectually with the idea, she didn't really want to actually live it and be responsible. When we pointed out the obvious truth that she agreed with the concept of being responsible but she didn't like being the responsible party, Charlotte cracked a smile and chuckled. "No, I don't like that," she said. "No."

As the laughter settled, Ariel proposed that Charlotte had dressed up her two-year-old's idea of independence, Don't Tell Me What To Do, in a more "adult" philosophy: Feminism. "You don't want to be waiting on Bill," Ariel said with a smile. "After all, what kind of person would that make *you*...you subservient wench!"

"Perhaps," Charlotte suggested, "I could just go and stand by the door and wait for him."

On the surface, this suggestion might seem like Charlotte had ended the fight, no longer punishing Bill by making him wait for her again. But in truth, this idea is really the flip side of the same coin. Making your partner aware that you are waiting, probably while tapping your foot and checking your watch, is just another way of putting pressure on him or her to finish up quickly and get out the door. It's a way of seeming to be supportive, to allow them to do whatever it is they're doing, but at the same time you're making them pay for it, so it's not really supportive at all. If you're suffering through your partner's actions, that's just another form of fighting.

Shya gave Charlotte another example of what waiting for each other can be like when you're not conflicted. "We live out here in New Jersey," said Shya, "and we have to drive an hour or so into New York City to lead our seminars on Monday nights. Frequently, Ariel is putting on her makeup and I'm ready to go. When this is the case, what I normally do is put things in the car that need to go with us. I just get everything prepared. I make sure the doors are locked, lights are out and everything is set. Then we can leave when she's done rather than my complaining about her putting on her makeup. Also, since it takes Ariel a bit longer than it does for me, she tends to get started earlier. This way we can time things to be ready around the same time."

"You know," Shya said to Charlotte, "surrender is cool.

Really. It allows both of you to win."

Charlotte looked at him, nodding, her eyes bright, as though she had just heard this simple truth for the first time. "So we both win," she said. "That's great."

 100% Responsibility
TransformationMadeEasy.com/matchmadeinheaven

SURRENDER VS. SUCCUMB

Our definition of surrender is when you do what is asked of you as though it was your idea in the first place. You intend for it to work out and you do it as though it's a great idea. This way you're in charge rather than dragging your feet because your partner suggested it. If you operate with the intention of having a wonderful time with whatever your partner wants to do and you really enjoy doing it, you're both happy.

How many times have you said, "Yes," to what is requested of you and then resented that you had to do it? Our definition of succumbing is doing what is asked of you but while doing it, proving that he or she made a mistake in asking you in the first place. This is another version of fighting: not having fun, being a victim and proving him or her wrong in the process. It's a subtle (or not so subtle) way of trying to prove your point of view to be the superior one or trying to make your partner suffer.

True surrender allows you both to win. You'll experience well-being because you've really said "yes" to your life and embraced it 100% without holding back. Your partner will feel well in himself or herself because he or she has you as a partner. Saying "yes" to your life sets the stage for happiness. When you're both happy, your relationship will thrive.

BEING RIGHT VS. BEING ALIVE REVISITED

We've already mentioned how the desire to be right about your point of view is one of the biggest relationship killers. For this reason it bears repeating many times. The dynamic can play out as a subtle, sneaky one, a not-so-distant cousin to succumbing to your partner. In other words, when you're being right that they are wrong, sometimes you do it silently. You're actually pretending to surrender while in the background you're still committed to hanging on to your point of view.

Here's an example of how it works and how it can transform.

ARIEL AT A CROSSROADS

It was a Friday afternoon and Shya and I were driving into New York City to begin one of our Transformational weekend seminars. As is our practice, we allowed ourselves plenty of travel time in case the traffic was heavy. But on this particular day there was an accident on the road that made the trip significantly longer than usual.

Originally we had intended to drive by the hotel, check in, then continue on to the workshop location, park the car near the venue and have a quick dinner before the course. But as we were driving into the Lincoln Tunnel, which runs under the Hudson River between New Jersey and New York, it was much later than we had anticipated. It was time to reevaluate our plans.

Shya was of the opinion that we could get it all done. I thought it was safer to skip the hotel and check in after the evening session. The only problem with my idea was that when we had checked in late in the past, often the only rooms left were the noisy ones by the ice machine or the elevator. There had even been an instance when the hotel had overbooked and had absolutely no rooms left when we arrived. They sent us to a different hotel, which made for a very late evening.

Even so, I was concerned about the traffic. Going across town in Manhattan on a Friday evening can sometimes be a very slow process. We know this from experience. I thought it safest to go directly to the parking lot near the course. In fact, I was fairly sure that would be the best way to go.

As we approached the end of the tunnel, we reached a crossroads—literally and figuratively. If we went to the seminar venue, we needed to turn right. If we went to the hotel first, we needed to turn left. I was concerned about our timing and so my vote was to go downtown to the seminar when Shya said to me again, "Ariel, we can get it all done. Let's go by the hotel."

"Okay," I said.

In that moment I realized I was at my own personal crossroads, too. It would have been easy to go along with Shya's plan but quietly, privately, secretly hold onto my own idea. I recognized as we made the left to head to the hotel, it would be almost natural to watch for Shya's plan to fail. I could easily have surreptitiously looked to be right. If we turned down a block that had a traffic backup or if we missed a light and had to sit for an extra moment or two at a red light, my original idea would have proved to be the superior one. If I didn't truly surrender to Shya's point of view, I would mentally be rooting for a delay in order to prove that my perspective was right after all. Shya would have to lose in order for me to win. But I would lose also since I'd have to be late for our seminar in order to be right. I turned the "alive" way, going in the direction our car was traveling rather than mentally being against it. It meant that if for some unforeseen reason we didn't have time for dinner before work, it would have been my plan, my choice, and I wouldn't be victimized by the circumstances.

As I surrendered to going to the hotel first as though it was my idea, I intended this to be an excellent choice, and I noticed how a sense of calm settled in. I was able to enjoy the ride. I placed a hand on Shya's leg and felt his warmth through the fabric of his pants. I watched people hurrying to their destinations. I could see lane openings ahead on my side of the car that couldn't be seen from the driver's seat and I acted as a co-pilot, partnering Shya in getting to our destination. I felt my shoulders and face relax. I was instantaneously in sync with Shya, the traffic, my environment and of course, my life.

It was a simple event, yet profound. I could see how in the basic enculturation process, we're taught to either fight or give in, but rarely how to partner. Both fighting and giving in are about being right. If I didn't wholeheartedly choose to do what I was actually doing (i.e., going to the hotel first), then I would be a victim of my life in general and of Shya in specific.

Shya and I are rather practiced at surrendering to each other. When one of us has a strong opinion for (or against) something, the other generally defers as if we were the originator of the action, not the follower. And yet, even though this has been our style of operating for many years, I had never before so clearly seen the choice, the crossroads, where one road led to tension and separation and the other led to intimacy.

Shya was accurate, by the way. Or perhaps it is more true to say we were accurate. We did have enough time to go to the hotel first and get it all done. We checked in, got a lovely room, drove downtown, enjoyed a bite to eat and arrived at the seminar relaxed and refreshed. All it took was going down the Alive road rather than the Right one. And guess what? If we had guessed incorrectly and hadn't had time for dinner, we would have enjoyed getting hungry and having our meal later.

> When you're going about your life (and your relationship) as if it's your idea, as if you're doing exactly what you want, your life and your relationship are heavenly indeed.

19

VALENTINE'S DAY

*I*n the final section on Being Right vs. Being Alive, we meet Caitlin, a beautiful young woman with bright eyes, who has been taking our workshops for a number of years. When Caitlin discovered us, she was single and, like most people, didn't know how to create a satisfying and fulfilling relationship. When she first met her husband, Rod, she fell in love, but they did not automatically have a Match Made in Heaven. However, through their commitment to having a magical relationship and courage to keep looking and telling the truth, Caitlin and Rod's marriage is now heavenly.

As we mentioned in the previous two chapters, learning how to surrender and giving up the need and desire to be right while embracing responsibility for the state of your relationship are fundamental to the foundation of having a Match Made in Heaven. But often they are the principles that people have the most difficulty putting into practice. This is why we have dedicated three chapters to explaining them.

We are about to see Caitlin's brilliant demonstration of surrendering to her husband's point of view and, albeit reluctantly at first, giving up being right. In doing so, she takes full responsibility for the well-being of her relationship. As a result, she gets to experience full self-expression, aliveness, health, happiness and intimacy with her husband.

HOLDING ONTO YOUR POINT OF VIEW

Our Monday Night Alive! seminar in New York City fell on Valentine's Day, so we thought it was a perfect opportunity to have an event devoted to relationships. During that evening, topics ranged from dating to divorce, from sexual intimacy to doing chores around the home. Of all the lively interactions we had with participants, one in particular stands out as being filled with humor, compassion and honesty. It was a bright moment of possibility for all those who were in attendance.

Shya was in the midst of talking to a woman about being willing to give up her attachment to her perspective so she could hear another person's point of view. The truth is, you can't truly hear what your partner is saying if you are holding onto your point of view. (No two things can occupy the same space at the same time: Second Principle of Instantaneous Transformation.) Caitlin jumped up to "call one on herself." She came to the front of the room and volunteered to reveal how devoted she had been to proving herself right. She had been sure that her perspective was the best one, the only one, and she had been positive that her husband Rod was wrong. They had been fighting, once again, about that very monumental and important topic: Washing the dishes. Join us in our lively interaction.

BEING RIGHT ABOUT THE DISHES

Caitlin was wearing a black leather jacket over a gauzy shirt, black pants and boots. Her straight dark blond hair gleamed as she strode to the front of the room in purposeful movements. Smiling in a way that suggested she was enjoying a quiet joke with herself, she announced, "My name's Caitlin and I had a disagreement with my husband about the dishes. It was kind of funny because I think when you're doing dishes you should use a lot of soap in order to get the dishes clean. He's of the opinion that soap comes as a concentrate and you only need a little bit that you put not on the dish, but on the sponge. Then you add water to the sponge and you can do a larger number of dishes that way, right?"

She paused for a moment as if to make sure that the audience was following her. Her delivery was perfect. She had seen her steadfast desire to be right and had come through to the other side. She was close enough to the experience that she could communicate the seriousness with which she had approached the subject while poking fun at her earlier attitude.

"My point was that his way was *wrong*. Not only was it wrong, but he was going to make us sick if he did the dishes that way because they weren't going to actually get clean. So today we ran out of dish soap and we only had a little. I said to myself, 'Huh, I can just not do the dishes or I have to go out and get dish soap or I could try what he said...but I'm not going to tell him.'"

We all laughed. She was willing to test the possibility that her husband's idea had merit but initially she wanted to do it in secret. That way she wouldn't have to let him know she had backed down from her stubborn stance that in order to get dishes truly clean, you had to put soap on each and every individual dish.

"So I added some water to the dish soap and then I put it on the sponge..." Like a magician who has just pulled off a marvelous trick, she looked at us all as if to say, "Ta-Da!"

We laughed as she continued, "I was absolutely certain that he was absolutely wrong! But doing it his way with just a little of the remaining dish soap, I finished them. The other night I was not willing to see that, well, he might actually be accurate. That wasn't an option."

Caitlin's brilliance was shining through her attitude of mock seriousness that highlighted how she had been treating the subject of soap and dishes with critical importance. This was a perfect time to talk about being Right vs. being Alive, so Shya took the lead.

"In life," he said, "there are two possibilities. You can either be right about your point of view or you can have the experience of love, health, happiness, full self-expression, relationship, partnership and things like that. When you were being right that he was wrong about the soap, about how to wash dishes, how much of an experience of love did you have for your husband?"

"Not much," she said.

"Okay, not much," Shya continued. "How healthy was your relationship in that moment?"

"We were fighting."

"Happiness. How much happiness existed between you in that moment?"

"None," she said.

"How about your full self-expression?"

"Well, I was right."

"You were right," Shya said hanging his head as if this was really sad news. Everyone laughed with Caitlin and empathized. Each of us had at one time or anther fallen prey to the need to be right over silly things, which in the moment that the argument took place had seemed monumental.

The two of them were on a roll now. As if it were a friendly ping-pong exhibition, Shya kept tapping the ball over the net and Caitlin kept lobbing it back.

"But were you fully self-expressive?"

"Only about being right," she said.

"Only about being right, very good," Shya reiterated. "How was your partnership in that moment?"

"It didn't exist."

"It didn't exist, right." Shya turned, addressing everyone assembled in the room, "Now you have a possibility of being Right or being Alive. Our definition of aliveness is the experience of health, happiness, love, full self-expression, relationship and partnership. Okay?"

Heads nodded and he continued, "In life you have two possibilities. You have the possibility of being right or you have the possibility of the experience of aliveness. But you can't have both at the same time. In life, there's rent to pay. See, you can live in the Right house and there's rent to pay or you can live in the Alive house and there's rent to pay. The cost of living in the Alive house is you have to give up being right. The cost of living in the Right house is you have to give up your experience of aliveness. It's that simple. Each of you has the right to mechanically disagree with your partner. But it will rob you of your experience of aliveness. It will absolutely not have you feeling more cuddly."

Heads nodded. Folks chuckled.

"In fact, you'll move to opposite sides of the bed, backs to each other, faces to the wall."

"Yes!" Caitlin grinned, her face filling with delight. It was obvious that she and her husband Rod had been so invested in petty arguments in the past, they had gone to sleep in just such a manner.

"Yes, and that's the way it went over dishwashing soap," Shya said.

Folks laughed at the absurdity of the situation and at the realization that many had been party to just such a fight.

"It's so stupid," Caitlin said.

"I know it's so stupid," Shya replied. "But when you're

locked in this type of dynamic, you're 'right,' he's 'wrong.' Pick any topic and it will be the same."

BEING A "YES" TO YOURSELF FIRST

With Charlotte, we saw the significance of surrendering and how you can't create a Match Made in Heaven without it. But being a "yes" to your partner's requests, ideas or ways of being starts with being a "yes" to yourself and your environment.

Many people struggle with this, finding it difficult not to complain to themselves about having to do something and resist doing it. As we saw with Nisha, who didn't want to do the dishes even if it meant greater well-being in her life and relationship, the dictate of Don't Tell Me What to Do can dominate our lives and prevent us from surrendering to our lives, our partners and ourselves. Of course, it doesn't have to. We always have a choice. If we do leave behind this mechanical behavior, we are free. Otherwise we're stuck in saying "no" to everything and not doing what we need to do, even if we're telling ourselves to do it!

Caitlin gave us an excellent example of seeing her mechanical "no" to her husband and then letting it go and stepping into partnership with him. But she hadn't yet made the link between this and saying "yes" to herself. Ariel offered an example of how being a "yes" to herself and to the requests her environment makes, translates directly into being a "yes" to Shya:

"We've gotten to a place where I can say 'yes' to a request to myself so it's easy to say 'yes' to Shya's requests. I'll give you an example. One of the things Shya and I do for recreation is offshore fishing. When we were in Costa Rica, we went offshore to hunt for giant sailfish and marlin and tuna and whatever else was out there. We fish with fly rods, so the fish have a real fighting chance, and it's something we've had a lot of fun doing. But we hadn't done it in a number of years.

"One of the things that happens when you get out there, particularly nowadays, is there aren't that many fish around. You can go out for eight hours and, when you get really offshore, you can't see where land is. There's this expanse of water and nothing but sun. I'm rather sensitive to the sun. The challenge of being on a boat in the middle of the ocean under a sunny sky is that there's a lot of sun and very little shade. The deal with this type of fishing is that the boat doesn't go in a straight line. It zigzags and goes in circles. So just when you get comfortably in a shady position where you have no boat fumes, it turns. You have to pick up your behind and move with it.

"In the past I would get comfortable, then the sun would come and I would sigh, and it was such a big deal to move. But what I noticed this year was: sun, move, sun, move.... It was not this big imposition to have to cross the boat. If I had the impulse to move, I followed my impulse without having to talk to myself about whether or not I wanted to do it. I didn't have to negotiate with myself: *Do I want to get up yet? Well, I can handle five minutes in the sun before I really bake.*

"There was a 'yes' to me, to the requests of my universe, and it translates directly to Shya. If he asks me for something, it's not an imposition either. Even in the middle of the night. He'll talk to me and ask me to massage a spot on his back if it's hurting him. It's always a 'yes' if I'm awake to hear it. It really starts with me, with being a 'yes' to me."

BEING A "YES" TO YOUR "NO": AUTHENTIC VS. AUTOMATIC

When we talk about surrendering to your partner and the circumstances of your life in general, we are not sug-

gesting that in order to have well-being you have to say
"yes" to absolutely everything without discrimination.
There are times when you'll be a genuine "no." Not because you're acting out a fight, succumbing to your mechanical Don't Tell Me What to Do nature, being lazy or
complaining that you're "not in the mood," but simply
because you know, authentically, that it isn't right for
you to say "yes" to the request in that moment.

This is not the same thing as an automatic "no," such
as when your partner asks if you want to go to the movies
and, without even thinking, you say, "No, what's playing?" If your automatic "no" is deeply ingrained within
you, at first it might be a little tricky finding your authentic "no." You need to become well practiced at surrendering and saying "yes" before you know that your
"no" is authentic, not automatic. To demonstrate this
dynamic, Ariel gave an example of how she and Shya
operate at home:

"If I ask Shya to make me a cup of coffee," she said,
"generally it doesn't matter what he's doing. He'll set it
down and make a cup for me. If you get accomplished
at saying 'yes' to your life, you become really clear when
'no' is authentic. If I ask Shya to make me a cup of coffee
and he says, 'No, I'm in the midst of something,' I know
it isn't simply an automatic response. I know he's in the
midst of something. Then I'm a 'yes' to his 'no.'"

SOCIALIZED INTO FIGHTING
Since we take an anthropological view of life, we recognize that Caitlin, along with everybody else on the planet,
was raised by people who passed on their way of behaving to the next generation. She absorbed her parents' way
of relating along with the language she learned to speak.
In turn, her parents were raised by people who taught
them their way of behaving. And so on, from generation

to generation. These people were all well-meaning but they lived difficult lives according to rules of behavior that were often harsh. They learned to fight to survive.

Caitlin wasn't really fighting about soap and dishes. She had learned to fight. She had learned that if she actually listened to her husband's point of view (about the optimal amount of soap to use while washing dishes) and tried it to see if he was accurate, she would lose her independence. Socialized into this way of being, Caitlin assumed that if her husband suggested something other than her pre-existing point of view, he had to be wrong.

Since most of us were similarly brought up, this is a normal way of behaving in relationships. If whatever our partner says doesn't automatically agree with what we know or assume to be true, we see it as something to be viewed with skepticism. We see it as fodder for disagreement. We learn to disagree as a way of life. And we carry that way of being into our relationships, acting it out even when the topic is as silly as how to wash a dish.

Caitlin couldn't stop laughing while we spoke with her. She recognized the truth and saw herself in everything we said. She even admitted that Rod had volunteered to do the dishes but she had said no. "I don't know why I argued with him," she exclaimed, seeing how the urge to fight even got in the way of what she actually wanted.

"Because you've been socialized to argue," Shya reminded her. "Who's going to run your life: the socialization process you were inculcated in initially or the adult woman you've become?" He then told her that it was entirely her choice. But in order to be fully in control of her life—instead of letting ancient familial mechanical behaviors take over—she had to be consistently willing to give up her point of view. Only then would she have a choice about how to act, because free choice does not exist when you're being right.

FIGHTING AS AVOIDANCE

One last piece of the puzzle we pointed out to Caitlin was that she tended to pick a fight with her husband when she was experiencing uncertainty. For example, she would pick a fight when she was waiting to hear if she'd gotten a job. Caitlin is an internationally successful costume designer and the nature of her work means that she is not permanently employed. If she became stressed while waiting, Caitlin would pick a fight with Rod to avoid being in the unknown and feeling the discomfort of uncertainty. For Caitlin, in those moments, the stress of fighting was less than the stress of not knowing where her next job was coming from. Fighting kept her occupied and her mind distracted from that discomfort.

While you may not have similar life circumstances to Caitlin, it is certainly possible that you use fighting as a way of avoiding other feelings or experiences that you are less comfortable with. Intimacy, for example.

Many of us were raised in households where arguing was far more acceptable than displays of affection, where fighting was more easily tolerated than intimacy. When this is the case, it's hardly surprising that your comfort zone is in a fight. But once you start to recognize the habits and behaviors that have been socialized into you, you can make different choices.

 Being Right About the Dishes
TransformationMadeEasy.com/matchmadeinheaven

TRANSFORMING YOUR RELATIONSHIP

In these last three chapters we have seen how three different women approached their relationships. Nisha, having just learned about "being Right vs. being Alive" and "surrender vs. succumb" was curious about the possibilities, for both personal well-being and increased intimacy with her boyfriend. But she was still too wedded to her own point of view and the desire to be right to overcome her mechanical behaviors and surrender to her boyfriend and herself. She held the possibility as an option but it wasn't one she was choosing just yet.

Charlotte was quite committed to a transformational approach in her relationship with her husband. As a result, they had a very successful partnership filled with far more intimacy and well-being than it ever had before. But they still had potential for experiencing even greater levels of intimacy and partnership together. These levels weren't being reached when Charlotte was attached to her point of view and her reluctance to be completely responsible for her relationship. She still wanted to share the responsibility with Bill 50-50 and that sabotaged the well-being of their marriage.

Caitlin could see her reflexive resistance to listening to her husband's point of view, which had been socialized into her. She discovered her desire to be right and her reluctance to surrender. She could feel how ingrained those mechanical behaviors were. But with willingness, humor and awareness, she was able to override her automatic nature and choose a different path. She could put down her point of view, albeit reluctantly at first, and test out her husband's way of seeing. When she realized how accurate he was, she laughed at herself and experienced true intimacy and aliveness.

Had the conversations we had with these three ladies taken place with their partners, we would have encour-

aged each of the men to be 100% responsible for the
health and well-being of their relationship, too. Whether
you are a man or a woman, ultimately the quality of your
relationship is a reflection of your willingness to be the
responsible party.

20

UN-INDEPENDENCE DAY

*I*n our seminars we have the privilege to meet many remarkable individuals. One such person is Frannie. She is a witty, smart, lively woman in her mid-60s. She has shoulder-length grey hair that somehow looks less like a sign of age and more like a color chosen by someone with good fashion sense.

On the day that Frannie called into our Internet radio show, *Being Here,* we had only known her for a few months. She was relatively new to our ideas but she had already started to open up to the possibilities that her life had to offer. Join us as we have a simple conversation with Frannie that reveals a lifelong way of relating that has had a profound impact on her ability to be with people.

"Hi Frannie," Ariel began. "What can we do for you?"

"Well in a nutshell, I've never really had a relationship that worked and I think it's still possible for me, but I don't have one now," Frannie said in a voice that betrayed her frustration.

"Well, you've got to slow down a little bit, Frannie," Shya said. "Where did you get the idea that you have to have a relationship?"

"I can't ever remember not thinking that."

171

"Give us an idea of your age," Ariel said.

"I'm 65."

"We know you, so we know that you have the qualities that could allow you to have a relationship, should you want one," Shya said. "But I have the idea that you *think* you want a relationship more than you actually do in reality. What I mean by that is that over the years, you've had the opportunity to have relationships, or the opportunity to start forming one but something else seemed more important."

"Could be my independence," Frannie said.

"Right. Exactly. Especially in the years that you grew up, to be a whole person, you didn't want to be…" Shya paused while searching for the word that best described what Frannie had been eager to avoid in her youth.

"Subjugated," Ariel said.

"Subjugated. Right," Shya confirmed. "You didn't want to give over your independence to a man."

"Yeah," Frannie admitted.

"And you didn't want to give up your right to be *your* person." Shya said.

"And somehow I think I do have to do that."

"Well on some level if you're in a relationship you do. There is this thing called 'surrender.'" Shya said.

"Ahh," Frannie said. That one short syllable held a wealth of meaning. The word "ahh" was short and clipped as if her worst fears had been confirmed, as if we had just given her bad news. In Frannie's mind we had validated her idea that in order to have a relationship she would have to lose herself, become less and give up her cherished independence. She was afraid that if she surrendered, she would be a prisoner to her partner's desires, subjugated to his whims. This was indeed in her mind, a prison sentence that she was unwilling to serve.

"Surrender isn't like waving a white flag saying, 'I give

up,'" Ariel said. "It isn't 'You win, I lose.'"

"Yes," Shya said. "Our definition of surrender is choosing to have what you have in your life like it's your idea. You choose it as if it was your idea to begin with, not something that someone else is imposing on you, not something you succumb to and complain about and wish were different than it is."

"Oh," Frannie said, sounding slightly nauseated.

"Most of the people I've met succumb rather than surrender to their lives," Shya said. "What we're speaking about here, Frannie, is surrender-versus-succumb. Not in relation to relationship *per se*. We're actually speaking about how one deals with each moment of his or her life. In each moment you have this choice: You can either surrender and be a 'yes' to how your life is showing up, whether it meets your ideals or not, or you can succumb and be the victim of the circumstances of your life. I daresay most of us were trained by people who were victimized by their lives. They didn't see their own successes.

"For example, last week at our NYC group, Monday Night Alive!, there was a very lovely young lady whose name is Christina. She said she was training to run The New York City Marathon and she had just completed a 20-mile run in preparation for it. She told us that after running about 17 miles she started to feel pain in her body yet she pushed through it and completed the full practice run. But Christina still felt like a failure because she'd–'only run 20 miles'–only 20 miles. That's an amazing accomplishment.

"But she had missed the incredible nature of it because she was going somewhere, aiming toward her goal. This run wasn't the way she would have preferred it to be. She had an idea in advance that if she was ready, she shouldn't have any difficulty. Since she hit a patch of difficulty at 17 miles it wasn't good enough.

"Many of us have preferences about how our lives should be and what our life circumstances should be like. We compare where we think we should be to how our life is showing up. Life doesn't fit those ideals because life doesn't really care what you want. It just goes along the way it does. The game is to be a 'yes' to how your life is," Shya said.

"So, Frannie, are you still with us?" Ariel asked.

"I am," Frannie said. "I'm really liking this. I'm seeing that if I just agree, if I just say 'Yes, that was my choice,' then I'm a whole lot less likely to be a victim of my circumstances."

"True," Shya said. "If you look, you'll see that in every moment of your life, you've done exactly what you've done and you weren't wrong."

"You know," Ariel said, "Shya and I haven't known you for very long, Frannie, but in the relatively short time we've become friendly with you on Mondays and weekends, I see you as far more able to have a relationship now, should you want one because you are so much more accessible these days. You used to habitually take an opposing side to whatever was happening. It really didn't matter what the circumstances were. You had developed a persona of 'the little devil maker,' as if this was fun. This reflexive way of relating actually was quite fun some of the time, but I don't think that a relationship would sustain a lot of that if you want to create intimacy with another person."

"I think that's a good point," Frannie said. "Now that you mention it, I'm thinking of how elections were handled in my family growing up. Whoever my mother voted for, my father would vote for the other guy."

Shya laughed as he exclaimed, "I love it!"

"So I come from a long line of taking the other point

of view," Frannie said.

"Yeah," Shya said "You learned to take the other position."

"Well how cool is that?" Ariel asked.

We were both delighted that Frannie had seen the wiring for the button that initiated a fight—whether she wanted one or not. In her childhood, her primary role models for "love" included being on opposing sides in virtually any conversation. Unbeknownst to Frannie, she had carried this schematic for relating into all of her relationships—both casual and intimate. Chances are that the more she liked someone, the more she would feel compelled to play devil's advocate.

"Now that you see how your folks related," said Shya, "this gives you an amazing insight into your own behavior because for the most part, Frannie, you were programmed by your parents' behavior in the first six years of your life."

"Mmm," Frannie said warmly.

"You watched how they interacted and you made choices and decisions from seeing those interactions that went forward in time," Shya said. "If your father disagreed with your mother around elections, that was not the only point of contention."

"No, sir!" Frannie agreed.

"That's right. Then you learned to disagree as a lifestyle, a way of going about surviving," Shya said.

"You also probably saw who was winning and who was losing according to your young and immature mind," Ariel said. "You didn't recognize that this was a dynamic between them. It was a way of relating that they had fabricated together. And you likely chose sides. You didn't want to be like the one that you found most..."

"Acquiescent," Frannie said.

"Acquiescent, very good word." Ariel replied.

Frannie had obviously grown up in a win/lose atmo-
sphere and she hadn't wanted to be on the losing side of
any situation. She learned that to yield to another's perspective would be to lose, acquiesce, to be submissive, to
be less. As a child she had never seen a Transformational
Approach to Dating, Relating and Marriage.

Frannie's parents certainly didn't know about True Listening. They didn't realize that to actually listen to hear
something from your husband or wife's perspective was
really a gift to yourself and to your partner. They didn't
know that it was possible for *both* parties to win. When
you truly listen to another, you have to fully let go of
your point of view. This doesn't make you weak. This
doesn't make you a doormat. It doesn't make you subservient, either. It takes a strong person who is secure in
him- or herself to let go of what he or she wants to say in
order to fully hear another.

Frannie had grown up in a climate where someone was
always on top and the other was always subjugated—one
where her parents were in a constant struggle for domi-
nance.

"Perfect," Shya said. "You just solved the puzzle of
your own relationship to relationship."

"Simple as that," Frannie said.

"As simple as that," Shya replied.

"Now here's the challenge," Ariel said. "You have both
sides of that fight inside of you with *you*."

"Hmm," Frannie said, intrigued by what Ariel had just
told her.

"When you go to work and you have the impulse to do
one thing, you may also take the opposing side and find
yourself procrastinating."

"Oh, very interesting," Frannie said.

"But that's not a problem if you see it," Shya continued. "If you see it, you can override the mechanism. You

have ultimate power in your life. You are God in your own universe."

"You know, Frannie," Ariel said, "one thing I've always admired about you from the first night you stood up during one of our seminars and spoke, was your tenacity. I have admired your ability to take a stand and put forth something. I think that this tenacity is going to stand you in really good stead as you look at dissolving the mechanical behaviors in your life, should you be willing to. All you have to do is not judge what you see."

"I know that you attend our Monday Night Alive! seminars in New York and you've seen people like Holly and John," Shya said. "For years Holly didn't have a relationship and for more years than that John didn't have one either. Now they're quite happy with each other in a very lovely relationship. But it took a while until they rubbed off their rough edges. You know, a relationship is a lot like a rock-polishing machine."

"You hop inside, it turns, and you bump off the rough edges until you become polished," Ariel said.

Frannie laughed at the imagery.

"I have a question for you," Ariel said.

"Yeah?"

"In this moment, how are you feeling about yourself?"

"I'm delighted actually. I'm smiling a big smile."

"Well guess what," said Ariel. "You just created a fabulous relationship with yourself."

"Oh!" Frannie said.

"And if you have one of those with yourself…"

"You can have a relationship with another," Shya said. "You see, Frannie, it's when people aren't aware of their own impediments to relating to themselves, when they're hard on and not nice to themselves, they bring that kind of behavior into any relationship they get into. You could find the perfect person, but if you're still committed to being right and proving your point of view over anything else, that commitment to righteousness will destroy any relationship."

"I believe you," Frannie said. She could easily see the truth of his statement by looking at her own life.

"Relationship really is about listening," Shya said. "We talked about listening at the beginning of this radio show. We talk about listening at the top of every show. Listening is truly key to having a magical life and that includes a magical relationship."

"I have another question for you," Ariel said. "Are you coming to the Art of Listening, our New York City course in November?"

"I sure am," Frannie said.

"Perfect," Ariel said. "I'll tell you what I would love you to pay attention to between now and then because I think it's going to be so wonderful for you. You've been trained to look for the opposing side in any situation. It's automatic. It's internalized."

"Uh-hum," Frannie said.

"Your listening has been skewed that way," Ariel said. "When you listen to somebody, you look for the chinks, you look for the exception, you look for the inaccurate word. It would be really neat if you started listening from a win/win perspective where *you* win with what they say and you have *them* win with what they say rather than having to point out faults."

"Yeah," Frannie said. "Good plan."

"It makes me very excited for you," Ariel said, "because you've been trained in a win/lose modality. Transformation is win/win. You win, I win, Shya wins, the listeners win and everybody wins rather than somebody having to come out on the losing side. It's a whole new perspective."

"I'm grateful that you pointed out how deep this goes and how automatic it's been for me," Frannie said.

"If you see it, that's enough." Shya said. "Our technology is about an instantaneous shifting in your reality, not over time. You don't have to work on this. If you see it, it's enough—it's over. In that moment, it's over. And if it shows up again, if you see it again without judging it, it's over then, too."

"Not to take exception to what you just said, Frannie," Ariel said, "but you're the one who pointed out how deep it goes and how far back. You're the one who is brilliant enough to see it and willing to reveal it. That's amazing. That's like Christina running 20 miles but without the pain."

"Wow!" Frannie said.

"Excellent," Ariel replied. "Hey, thank you, Frannie, for calling in today."

"Yes, thank you," Shya said. "It's been such a pleasure having you on our show."

"I loved it!" Frannie said. "Thank you. See you next Monday!"

 These are the Good Old Days: Un-Independence Day
TransformationMadeEasy.com/matchmadeinheaven

21

THE BLAME GAME

*F*rannie's way of relating to life is not unusual. Many people have been raised in families that have an embattled mindset. In fact, it is so normal to most people that the reality of being on opposing "teams" is simply the background from which their relationships operate. Here is another example:

THE EMBATTLED MINDSET

We were once shopping at a local store and the owner, Carol, blurted out, "Do you lock your car while you're here?"

We replied, "Yes. Always."

Carol continued with what was obviously on her mind. "I don't lock mine and my GPS was stolen from my car," she said. "I didn't realize it at first, so I said to my husband, 'Jerry, why did you take my GPS from my car?' He said, 'I didn't touch your GPS!' Then I remembered something: A week earlier, I had heard a car door close in the parking lot. When I looked up from what I was doing, I saw someone standing near my car. At the time I didn't think much of it. Since I didn't need my GPS that day I didn't think about it, but later, I recalled that moment. I recognized that at the time, I had felt that something was off or wrong with the person who was in the parking lot near my car. Then I realized that this person must have taken it."

At that point we reiterated that as a matter of course we simply lock our car, even next to a small local business. It just supports keeping an honest person honest.

Carol replied, "That's what my husband always says."

What we found interesting was not the fact that Carol had been a victim of theft but how in her thoughts and actions, she automatically blamed her husband for the missing item. She didn't say, "Jerry, I can't find my GPS for some reason. Have you seen it?" Automatically, mechanically, the perpetrator must have been Jerry. When in doubt, blame your spouse.

We are certain that Carol didn't come up with this mindset by herself. In the early years she was enculturated into the Blame Game. Chances are she saw her mother relate in just such a manner. In many family units, the opposite gender is an adversary and the battle lines are clearly drawn. "If he says, 'do something,' then I do the opposite because it's my life, so don't tell me what to do."

It was clear from Carol's way of being that she hadn't given her attitude toward her husband a second thought. It was as if admitting to herself and to him that he was "right" about something would somehow be a great sacrifice. Her question to us about whether or not we lock our car was a loaded one. She wasn't actually looking for our perspective but rather was on a search to prove her point of view to be the correct one. She wanted to find others of a like mind so she could go back to her husband Jerry and let him know that "everyone" leaves their car unlocked and that she wasn't really irresponsible. Her question was a part of the fight and she hoped that we would be unwitting soldiers on her side of the dispute.

Carol had so internalized the gender war she had

absorbed while growing up, she didn't realize that her mindset was embattled and her husband was her adversary. Having known her for some time, we know that she genuinely loves Jerry. But we also know that her relationship is played out through an ongoing fight that is unexamined and not even of her own making. Her way of relating is, from her perspective, part of a "normal relationship."

If you want your relationship to be a Match Made in Heaven, it is imperative that you become interested in the attitudes you bring to it. It is often challenging to look at how you think and act because it might be embarrassing to see the real truth. But what if you were to take an anthropological approach to how you relate rather than a subjective, judgmental one? If you were a scientist, looking to see how the inner workings of a culture was put together, you would notate what you see—not judge it. If you bring an active interest, an observational approach to how you have been programmed, then you can "debug" your own personal computer.

Think of yourself as a highly sophisticated computer with archaic programming. Simple awareness acts like a complimentary upgrade.

If you take what you discover personally, as if you or someone else is to blame for what you find, you will have jumped right into a problem/solution/change paradigm rather than a transformational one. If you resist what you see about yourself, you will only reinforce the behavior and perhaps even hide from yourself what you consider a "bad" habit.

No one likes to see "bad" things about him- or herself. This is the First Principle of Instantaneous Transformation: What you resist persists and grows stronger and dominates your life. Carol's anecdote is a perfect example of this. She was resisting many things, such as her husband's suggestions to lock her car and the fact that her GPS was stolen. Weeks later her life was still dominated by the event.

The next thing about an anthropological approach is that in any given moment you can only be the way that you are. (The Second Principle of Instantaneous Transformation.) We each have many outdated attitudes and ways of relating. These relics of the past—unexamined behaviors that are frozen in place—have been handed down from generation to generation and absorbed during our formative years. They were set in place by younger, less astute versions of ourselves. Awareness truly is like exposing ice to the radiant heat of the sun. Ways of being that have been frozen in time can be transformed in an instant. This, of course, is the Third Principle of Instantaneous Transformation:

Anything you allow to be, allows you to be.

In other words, anything you see without judging completes itself and ceases to dominate your life.

If you don't know to look, you won't see.

If you want to keep your relationship alive and fresh and wondrous, keep paying attention to your attitudes toward yourself and toward your partner without working on what you discover or judging what you see.

Most, if not all, relationships start out with an embattled mindset. But with awareness, not only can you see where the battle lines have been drawn, you can also watch those lines fade away until they no longer exist.

22

NOTICE WHAT YOU'RE UP TO

*I*n this chapter we meet Val, a beautiful, bubbly young woman of Korean/American descent with soft black hair that sits just below her shoulders. Val works for us, so we know her both professionally and personally. We sat down together in our garden on a beautiful sunny day and Val began talking about how she found herself getting annoyed with people, especially those she liked.

"Anyone in particular?" Shya asked.

"Well," Val admitted, a little embarrassed, "my boyfriend."

"Yes," Shya said, "that's who I thought it was."

"Part of the reason," Ariel explained, "is that there are things you want him to do whether he wants to do them or not. And you disagree with him when he chooses to do something different. You're actually trying to force him to do the things you want him to do rather than the things he wants."

"Yes," Val nodded, "that's true."

"For example," Ariel continued, "I know you would have loved for him to come with you today. You would have loved the company and it would look good to other people. You have a picture of what being a boyfriend/girlfriend means, and the amount of time you should spend together, but he's not cooperating. He's playing a football game today. He's doing things other than what you want."

"Right," Val admitted, seeing her agenda. "That's it."

"But if you keep demanding that he do things he doesn't want to do, you'll force yourself out of the relationship," Ariel explained. "Which may be what you want."

"It doesn't feel like…" Val became a little flustered and confused, momentarily resisting the idea. "It's not what I want."

"You can only know what you want by noticing what you're doing," Ariel said. "Shya and I have been together for about three decades. That's a long time and it is never the same from moment to moment. I can look at whether I'm inviting him toward me or pushing him away by noticing how I'm behaving. When you say, 'Oh, it's not what I want,' that's because you're afraid to look at how you're being. It doesn't mean anything 'bad' if you are pushing him away. Just notice what you're up to."

Relationships are not static. They are always evolving. People often think that once you get married, the relationship is settled, solid and complete. But obviously that is not the case. If it were, there wouldn't be a 50% divorce rate in the United States. It's important that you pay attention to how you're being. If you see how you're being and take a look at your actions (without judging yourself for what you discover), you'll know whether you are pushing your partner away or inviting him closer.

"Okay," Val said, clearly grateful for the information. "Actually my boyfriend and I had a conversation yesterday about a lot of things. One thing we discussed is that he calls me sometimes just to say 'Hi.' I get annoyed with that, just that little thing. I hadn't seen that before."

"So," Ariel noticed the irony, "you want him around

more. But when he comes around more, you say, 'Honey, your timing sucks, go away.'"

We all laughed.

"It's not as though I'm doing anything really important," Val declared. "I'm just busy doing something I think I should be doing."

LEARNING A NEW LANGUAGE

"Neither one of you grew up in a culture of people who learned how to surrender to each other," Ariel explained. "I'm not casting aspersions on your family or his family. People in general don't know how to surrender to each other. You're learning a new skill set. It's a language."

"Sometimes," Shya said, "I need to put gas in my car. But I don't want to stop. Eventually I get the gas, but many times I don't stop to deal with what needs to be done because I'm going somewhere. You do that with your relationship. You're going somewhere and you want your boyfriend to get on board with your program."

"You work for us part-time," Ariel said. "I know that annoyance trigger in you because you've greeted me with it from time to time. But I've learned how to manage you. I say, 'Do you have a moment?' Then you have to choose if you want to talk to me or not. Then you say 'Yes,' or 'Can I call you back?' You're not really choosing when your boyfriend calls you. Maybe it's time to manage yourself."

"Right," Val agreed, able to see it clearly now without judging herself. "Thank you, that's great."

We sat back in our chairs, basking in the beauty of the garden and in Val's experience of transformation. At the beginning of the conversation, still unaware of her mechanical behaviors and social enculturation, Val couldn't see how she was sabotaging her relationship. She believed she wanted to be happy with her boyfriend but her behaviors were taking her in another direction. Now, with the simple awareness of seeing how she was acting and noticing the consequences those actions had on her relationship, Val was free to step outside her mechanical nature and drop her agendas. She could begin to surrender to her life and treat her boyfriend in ways that were conducive to having a Match Made in Heaven.

Notice What You're Up To
TransformationMadeEasy.com/matchmadeinheaven

23

THEY ARE NOT THE PROBLEM

*I*n this chapter we meet Menna and Artur, a couple who are now very happy together. She is English with fluffy blond hair and a fair complexion. He is Portuguese with a big smile, dark hair and eyes.

When we first met them several years ago, they were on the brink of divorce. At that time they had already been married six years and were worn down by fighting, their love slowly whittled away by hurtful thoughts, words and actions—both intended and unintended. As a last attempt to save their relationship, they attended one of our workshops in Hamburg, Germany. That weekend their lives and relationship transformed and they immediately signed up to join our Costa Rican Adventure, our immersion seminar into Instantaneous Transformation. Since then, they have regularly attended courses with us and it has been a delight to have them become close friends.

These days Menna and Artur have created a Match Made in Heaven of their own. Of course, they still stumble now and then when old mechanical behaviors momentarily seize control. In this chapter we see how Menna's old habit of blaming Artur returns, interrupting their intimacy and partnership.

"We've had the most incredible week here in Costa Rica," Menna began. "We've been relating so well and feeling really good with each other. And we've noticed that when things go off balance for us, as happened once this week, we automatically blame each other."

"Well, then," Shya said, "you've got it handled. If you can see that you automatically blame each other, then in that moment, you can stop doing it. It doesn't require a lot of strategy. What it requires is simply noticing that you're blaming each other. Or, from your point of view, that you're blaming Artur. And you can stop doing it. It's that simple. This is simple stuff."

"Part of where you're stuck," Ariel said, "is that you're judging yourself for automatically blaming Artur, or Artur for automatically blaming you. But notice the word *automatic*. It's not something you're in control of. It's a reflex. It's something that is pre-programmed. It means nothing.

"When we are very young, we learn how to walk, speak, tie our shoelaces, go to the restroom unaided, and how to relate to other people. We learn behaviors, attitudes and judgments that become ingrained until they're mechanical and automatic."

"In your enculturation process growing up," Shya said, "if there was ever a problem, you were always asked, 'What's wrong? What caused you to feel this way?' You learned to look outside yourself and find something or someone to blame your feelings on."

"My brother was mean to me," Ariel intoned in a childlike whine by way of example and Menna and Artur laughed.

"You're always looking for something outside of yourself to blame your upsets on," Shya said. "That's normal. Most people don't realize that they have a bundle of upsets always going on inside them and when they blame other things as the cause for those disturbances, that only keeps these upsets locked in place. Anything you resist persists and grows stronger—that's the First Principle of Instantaneous Transformation. The Second Principle is that you can only be exactly as you are in any given moment of your life—in any given moment of now. In this moment," Shya said, snapping his fingers, "if you were upset with each other, that's the only way you could be. It's an automatic thing."

Artur and Menna listened intently, nodding.

Shya continued, "When you can engage in self-observation without self reproach, where you start to notice objectively, 'Ah, look, I'm blaming Artur for feeling this way,' that's enough for that behavior to complete itself. That's the Third Principle: Anything you allow to be exactly as it is without judging it completes itself. It's very simple. If you see that you're blaming each other, that's a barometer showing you that you're off center, and then you can re-right yourself."

"It's not a problem, it's a symptom," Ariel explained, smiling. "You can see. 'Ah-ha, I'm upset.'"

AUTOMATIC THOUGHTS

"Yes," Artur said. "I think I've been seeing it as something negative about myself when I do that. So obviously, I've been keeping it in place."

"But when you say 'when I do that,' you are thinking that you do that." Ariel said. "In fact, this machine that each one of us has inside ourselves is what does it. You come along for the ride."

Artur laughed. "Right."

"You call that conversation 'you,'" Shya said. "But it's just a conversation taking place in your thoughts. Your thoughts are automatic and mechanical. I'll prove it to you. Think of a dog, right now. Did you get a picture?"

"Yes," Artur said. "I got a Dalmatian."

"Now, isn't that brilliant?" Shya said. "You didn't think to think of it, not really. It just popped up. I say 'dog' and you think of a Dalmatian. You could have seen a German Shepherd or a Chihuahua or a cat. Some people, contrary people, think of the opposite, so they get a cat when you say 'dog.' We all have an automatic thought process that is stimulated by our environment. You get stimulated by something, you get upset, and then your thought process immediately goes to blame, to figure out who caused this upset, since you think it couldn't be you."

"Especially if the thought itself triggers an emotion," Ariel added, "or a visceral response, a response in your body. Then it seems particularly real since you are experiencing all this agitation to prove it."

"Yes," Artur said, nodding while Menna smiled. Clearly they were both familiar with this.

YOU KNOW WHAT YOU WANT
BY HOW YOU ACT

"When I blame Artur, that's not what I want," Menna said. "It's what I automatically do but it's not what I want."

"Well, now we're getting into a tricky place," Shya said. "Because if you do it, then you want it. If you don't want to do it then you stop doing it.

"I remember once, many years ago, when I was being trained to lead seminars in a program in the Sierra Nevada Mountains. One day as I was preparing to go up on stage to lead a presentation, my manager came to the event and sat next to me. I said to him 'I'm nervous because you're here,' and he replied, 'Well, Shya, if you're nervous because I'm here and you know that, then stop being nervous.' I said, 'Okay, I can do that.' I had been blaming him for my nervousness but it really had nothing to do with him. I just wanted to get rid of him because I didn't want him to see me screw up somehow."

Ariel turned to Shya and said, "I got the funniest image in my mind a moment ago. You spoke about people being a bundle of upsets and I got the picture of a washing machine. Not a front-loading type, but the old fashioned kind. It has an agitator that washes the clothes. You have agitation inside, Menna. When one of your pieces of clothing (your upset) bobs to the surface, you can either believe that upset is you or realize that this agitation is just cleaning house. If you don't get involved in it, if you don't jump into the washing machine, if you simply notice it, then you will come out cleaner on the other side. If you believe this upset is you, you will in effect jump into the washing machine and you'll end up pretty bedraggled."

"Yes," Shya agreed, "you'll drown. That's what happens. People drown in their upsets. But it's a choice. To get upset is a choice, although most people don't realize that. Most people are upset and looking for something to blame their upset on. When they get a good justifier— something that seems acceptable to be upset or angry about—that's when they jump into their upset."

STAYING CENTERED

"There was a woman here in Costa Rica this week," Ariel said. "Her boyfriend whom she's lived with for many years has leukemia and he has a tumor that's pressing on his nerves so one of his legs keeps giving out on him. When he went to get out of bed the other morning, his leg wasn't working, but he didn't expect it, so he fell.

"His girlfriend helped him up and then he analyzed the situation. She told us that since his leg wasn't working, he asked himself how he could get out of bed without falling. The two of them were approaching the situation as an exploration, as an adventure rather than an upsetting event. It was so inspirational to hear about. Even in the midst of life-threatening situations, we are totally capable of being centered."

"What was amazing this week," Menna said, "was that in the past we would jump into our upsets more. But now we saw them as indulgences and it didn't take long at all, just a few minutes, before we snapped out of it. We have had such a week of partnership and togetherness, it made it so much easier to drop our upsets. Once, when I felt Artur blame me for something, I could feel the rush in my body and I wanted to defend myself. I felt like running away, that was my mechanical instinct. But I didn't act on it."

"Ah, yes," Ariel smiled. "But when you said, 'I felt Artur blaming me,' I could feel him tense up. In that moment you were re-poking the potential upset. In saying 'I wanted to run away because he was blaming me,' you were still blaming him."

"That's true," Menna said. She leaned into Artur and kissed his cheek. In turn he laughed and gave her a squeeze.

"Ah," Ariel smiled, "you two are great."

"I've had the most amazing time this week," Artur said. "I have never felt so well in myself. I could just be with people. I could be with whatever was there. It has been great."

"Wait," Ariel said, "it's just the beginning. It gets better. This is it and there is more to come."

"Thank you very much for providing this environment for us," Artur said.

"Our pleasure," Shya smiled.

"And we're looking forward to coming to England," Ariel said, "and hanging out with your friends."

"Yes, we're really looking forward to you coming," Menna grinned. "Thank you so much."

They Are Not the Problem
TransformationMadeEasy.com/matchmadeinheaven

NOW WHAT?

We were happy to see Menna and Artur so well grounded in their own personal centers, since life has a way of expanding and providing the next challenge once you've mastered any one aspect of it. Not long after our time together, Menna became pregnant and experienced the natural body changes, discomforts and hormones that one might anticipate, as well as some unexpected health challenges that required injections twice daily until she gave birth. Nine months after conception she had a healthy baby, a son they named Oscar. And a new chapter began, for as any parent knows, raising children can be one of the greatest stressors on any relationship.

A NEW LEVEL OF "SURRENDER"

In the months following the birth of their son, Oscar, Menna and Artur experienced many typical things that come along with being new parents: sleepless nights, a colicky baby, hourly feedings and the demands of an infant. Through it all the skill set of being present and having learned how to surrender to what is being requested by life stood them in good stead. They were able to meet their son's demands with humor. Surrendering is not only something that one does with one's partner. For Menna and Artur, it extended to nurturing their son as well.

Menna and Artur are in their own infancy when it comes to the process of raising a child, but they are very grateful for having a Transformational Approach to Dating, Relating, Marriage... and childrearing as well.

24

UNWIRING THE
TERRIBLE TWOS

During one of our workshops, our friends, Amy and Andy Gideon, brought their two-year-old son, Alex, with them. They were attending one of our Costa Rican Adventures. The challenge was that Alex was in the midst of a stage we like to call "The Terrible Twos." If the Gideons wanted Alex to walk with them, he would regularly run somewhere else. He would fly into a rage if they offered him Cheerios from a baggie rather than from the larger box. He threw his food. He had temper tantrums. In other words, he was exhibiting normal behavior for a two-year-old.

Over the course of several days we watched this dynamic unfold during breaks and meal times, as Alex had a babysitter when we were in session. We watched the family dynamics as anthropologists might, to observe how the culture of this family unit was put together, without judging what we saw.

One day, as all of the group participants sat down for lunch, Amy, Andy and Alex joined us at our table to enjoy a meal. But the meal turned out to be anything but enjoyable. Alex was acting up, screaming, banging the table, and throwing items around, leaving his parents embarrassed and exasperated as they tried their best to regain control. Finding someone to watch Alex, we took Amy and Andy aside and had a frank conversation.

Alex was not the problem, we told them. The way Amy and Andy related to each other was. As is normal in so many relationships, our friends were competing with each other, trying to prove who was the better parent. When Alex fussed about eating cereal that was in a baggie, Andrew said, "Amy, just give him the box!" When Andrew tried to make Alex sit at the table with them rather than crawl around on the floor, Amy said, "Oh Andy, just let him go where he wants."

In these scenarios, Alex was in control. At age two he had already become skilled at the "divide and conquer" game that children play in order to get their way. Usually this way of relating follows a child into later life. Remember Anne, whom we spoke about in a previous chapter on relationship splitters? It is virtually certain that her attempt to garner her father's attention to the exclusion of her mother had been set in place in her early childhood and reinforced by the way her parents related.

BEING AN ALLIED FRONT

We gave Amy and Andy some examples of what we had observed about their competitive natures. In fact, it didn't start with their relationship with Alex. It was something that was already woven into the fabric of their relationship from the start. Before Alex was born, we had seen them operating in a similar manner with their cat, Nicky, as they competed for his affection. Each wanted the family pet to love them the best!

Although it was a profoundly life-changing conversation, it wasn't heavy because the Gideons laughed when they saw the truth. It was as if a file had opened and they could see example after example of how their current way of relating affected all aspects of their lives and extended to how they parented.

We suggested to Amy and Andy that they get on the same page when it came to Alex. In other words, if one parent was taking an action, such as telling Alex that it was time to go to bed, the other should support it. If either of them had an idea of how to do things differently, it was important to have that conversation at a later time—not in front of their child. If Alex cried and said, "No! I want Mommy to put me to bed!" Amy should let him know that tonight Daddy was going to be in charge and that tomorrow she would put him to bed rather than be secretly pleased that Alex liked her best. Being an allied front, acting as a team, would give Alex stability and structure, two things that every child needs.

IF YOUR CHILD MISBEHAVES, GIVE YOUR-SELF A TIME OUT!

One other part of this brief but potent conversation had a dramatic effect on the Gideons' relationship and on the health of their children's lives. (They now have two boys!) This is the idea that kids act out when the parents are out of sync.

Children need proper nutrients and healthy meals, but they also need your love and attention. Kids thrive when you are fully interested in them. If you aren't present, a child will misbehave to get your attention. From a child's perspective, any attention, even the "bad" kind, is better than none. They need you. If you are always in the midst of emails, texting, conversations, television or other pursuits, they will often find a way to force you to see them and be with them. A temper tantrum can be an indicator that you aren't all there or that something is amiss between you and your partner.

Of course, children will be fussy when they are overtired, if something from school is bothering them, or when they are ill. But oftentimes they are reacting to the environment in which they are living. Long ago, coal miners would bring a canary with them down into the mines, as little birds are far more sensitive to noxious gases than humans are. If the canary stopped singing, it was time to get out! In the same way, our children are very sensitive and react to the tensions that crop up between parents or when a parent is out of sorts. If they stop "singing," you may want to look at how you are fighting or the toxins you are creating in the way you relate.

We have friends and clients with college-aged children who employed this strategy, not only when their kids were little but throughout the difficult teenage years as well. If their son or daughter slammed doors or defiantly played their music too loud, this couple would retreat to the kitchen or bedroom and look at their relationship, at what they had not been saying to each other and how they might be fighting. There is a funny old saying, "The fish stinks from the head down." As a result of our coaching, our friends realized that if they were out of sync as heads of the family, it would trickle down to their kids and create a stinky mess. Generally, when they identified how *they* were fighting and saw it without judging what they discovered, their kids would spontaneously transform right along with them.

ALEX'S TRANSFORMATION

After our conversation with Amy and Andy, we refilled our plates, returned to the table, and an amazing thing had happened. While we had been gone the little "beast" who was throwing his food and acting up had been replaced by a well-behaved young man. Alex was quiet and calm and it was as if suddenly we were sitting with three adults rather than a couple of exasperated parents and their unruly child. When a piece of food fell from

Alex's spoon, we asked if he would like a napkin. "Yes, please," he replied as he opened it and placed it gently across his lap. In an instant, Alex had become respectful, polite and well-mannered—a completely different boy.

Amy and Andy continue to be a team as they now parent both their children. It's a delight to see a Match Made in Heaven have a divine effect on an entire family.

25

LEARNING COMPASSION AND LETTING GO OF CHILDHOOD BEHAVIORS

Colleen is a bright, bubbly woman in her mid-40s with cropped brown hair, glasses and a stunning smile. Wearing a purple knit sweater and matching mauve earrings, she met us in our home as we sat in front of the fire in our living room to hear to what she had to say.

"I've been coming to your workshops for six years," Colleen quickly spoke up, "and one thing I'm always amazed and inspired by is your compassion and how you have space for people. My question: Is compassion a skill set or something you already have within you? Because I find that sometimes someone will be speaking and I'll be judging them."

"It's both. Yes, it's a skill set," Shya replied. "And yes, it's something that you already have within you. But it's a skill set that you can build on. If you have the desire for compassion, then you'll discover a way to be compassionate."

"It starts with you," Ariel said, "because the person you are least compassionate with is yourself and secondarily your husband because he's an extension of you. If you're going to get irritated by anyone, it will be with yourself first and him second."

"Or, when you don't want to take the blame for your own upset and anger," Shya added, "you'll blame him first and you second."

Colleen nodded. "That is so true, so true."

"The main thing is to start recognizing how you judge yourself and how you judge him," Ariel explained. "And how you can get tied up in a little knot around that."

"It starts with you being compassionate with yourself for your little foibles," said Shya, "the idiosyncrasies that you developed growing up in the culture you grew up in. You learned to be the way you are. You learned to be irritated with your spouse. It was an acceptable way of behaving in the family you grew up in, during the first six years of your life. People were less than kind to each other and they didn't think, 'We should not behave this way in front of the children.' That was simply the way they behaved. That was normal to them. And it became your schematic for a love relationship. Your schematic includes fighting, disagreeing and being right that he's wrong."

As Shya spoke, Colleen acknowledged this truth. "That's so true," she said, "and I've really been noticing that this week."

"That's great," Shya said. "The only problem with it is that you think you're wrong for having acted like that. Don't forget the Second Principle of Instantaneous Transformation, Colleen. In any given moment, you can only be exactly as you are. This also means that you could have only behaved the way you did."

"Yes," Colleen nodded.

"I saw this coming a week ago when you and I spoke at our Monday Night Alive! seminar," Ariel said. "We had a brief interaction only lasting about ten seconds. I asked you where your husband, Jay, was. You replied that he was working that night. But as you said it, you rolled your eyes and sighed. Because from time to time you want life to be different than it is. You want Jay to spend time with you. You want him to hang out, to do activities that you love to do together. But when he's working in the evening, he can't be with you because his schedule doesn't permit it. Then you get irritated and lonely. The strategy, from a child's point of view, is to have a temper tantrum, which of course, makes him oh-so-interested in being around you. Who likes being around a pouting child? You think you aren't getting enough quality time with Jay and your strategy to solve the situation is to give him 'The Face,'" Ariel laughed, mimicking a pouting child.

"Yes!" Colleen's face lit up as she recognized herself in Ariel's playfulness.

"If you come to Monday Night Alive! and then return to him in that pouting state, it doesn't inspire him to come with you the next time," Shya said. "Or to get off work early to spend time with you."

"That is my thought process," Colleen agreed, "that he could take time off work." As she spoke her smile fell, her lips tightening and her face hardening as it suddenly changed into that of an angry pouting child.

"Oh, I love your face!" Shya exclaimed. "I'm so glad we caught that on camera. That was great. You actually just dramatized what you present to him when he doesn't do what you think he should."

Colleen suddenly stopped and looked like a child who got caught being naughty. She tried to rearrange her features with only marginal success. It was easy to see the child she had been, superimposed over the woman she had become.

"How old is Jay?" Shya asked.

"He's 68."

"Is that old enough to know what he wants to do?"

Shya asked.

Colleen nodded.

"Maybe you should stop treating him like a child and stop acting like a child, and start behaving as grown-ups," Shya suggested.

"You work in a bank," Ariel added. "Imagine if I pouted and told you that you didn't have to go to work today and that you should take a day off to be with me. He just can't do that because he has his job."

"Yes," Colleen said as she recognized how unreasonable her demands had been. Her face brightened once more. "That's right," she said. "Thank you."

Compassion Begins with You
TransformationMadeEasy.com/matchmadeinheaven

CHILDHOOD STRATEGIES

Colleen's way of relating to her husband, Jay, is very typical in relationships. If you look at your own way of relating, you may see your variation of unattractive, childish attention-getting mechanisms. For example, have you ever gotten stiff and unavailable to your partner, giving him the cold shoulder when what you really wanted was to have him wrap his arms around you? Have you ever demanded that you are right about some silly point, all the while knowing that it didn't bring you closer as you continued to hold on to your point of view? Or like our client, Nisha, about whom we spoke earlier in the book, have you ever banged the pots and pans to indicate your displeasure, which actually produces nothing but more distance? Your childhood strategies for getting attention are not "bad." They are simply immature tactics employed by a younger version of you to get what you thought you wanted.

Once, the two of us visited a facility in upstate New York where we were contemplating renting space to lead some seminars. At the time it was being used as a summer camp for children aged 6 through 12. Cars were not allowed on the property so Tim, the camp manager, drove us around in an electric golf cart so we could see the different buildings. As we passed many children, each begged for a ride on the cart. It was funny to see immature strategies for success that were sure to follow these children into adulthood.

One small child pretended that he was a body builder and he struck a pose as if he was flexing his non-existent muscles, demanding in a pseudo-low, gruff voice, "Give me a ride on the cart!" Several girls were coy, striking a different type of pose as they batted their eyelashes and said, "Oh Tim, can I have a ride on your cart?" The young athletes jogged alongside as they made their plea. Others looked hurt and discouraged, their shoulders slumping, their heads hanging when Tim "rejected" them and kept on driving by. One little girl even lifted her dress as she made her request.

These types of childish strategies get more sophisticated and polished over time. Kids want what they want and lobby to get it even if what they want isn't good for them, isn't possible or isn't going to happen. Colleen hadn't recognized that getting sullen wasn't going to invite Jay to come closer. She hadn't seen that no matter how miserable she made herself, it just wasn't appropriate for Jay to be irresponsible and stay home from his job. It wouldn't have worked for her, either, to call the bank where she worked to say she wasn't coming in today because she felt like hanging out with her husband.

Once she saw that her "serious" face was that of a child wanting to get her way, she had the tools she needed to stop herself from having a temper tantrum. When she didn't judge herself for what saw, she was able to relax around the whole situation rather than drive Jay farther away by her need to be right. In an instant, the sullen face dissolved and the beautiful woman that she is shone through again.

26

DISTANT BUT CONNECTED

*I*n this chapter we meet Rod, a handsome man in his early 30s. Tall and lean with cropped blond hair and a wide smile, Rod is an actor recently married to a costume designer Caitlin whom we met in an earlier chapter. Their jobs frequently require that they spend time apart, sometimes for months in different parts of the world. He sat down to talk with us about the potential challenges of this situation.

"So," he began, "my wife is working out of town."

"Is it fun to say 'wife'?" Ariel asked with a smile. "How long have you been married?"

"Yes, it is," Rod grinned. "We've been married a year and a half now. She's currently working in Lithuania. I was recently in Rome doing a show and we got together there, which was great. But I noticed that after spending time apart when we came together again there was a period of adjustment, as though we had become strangers for a while."

"Well," Shya laughed, "that could be a very good thing."

"Yes, in that sense it is a very good thing," Rod nodded. "But I'm wondering how I can best take care of my wife when we're far apart."

"By being kind to yourself," Shya said. "If you're being kind to yourself, she'll be able to do what she is doing. This is because the two of you are connected, even at a distance. So if you're pulling on her energetically, pining for her in your thoughts, even though she's five thousand miles away, she'll feel it."

"I'll give you an example," Ariel said. "We have friends who moved to the West Coast that we haven't seen for a while. But a few days ago, Shya woke up and said, 'They're in trouble. I can feel them. They're in distress.'

"A few hours later they called us. We hadn't spoken to them in months and they called to give us some good news that had happened during the day. But we found out that they had been fighting when Shya spoke about them earlier. We could feel their distress, even at a distance."

DEVICES TO GET ATTENTION

"If your wife feels your distress, she'll be distracted. But perhaps that's what you want," Ariel suggested, "to get her attention."

"Yes, I've noticed that," Rod said earnestly. "We talk via Skype on the Internet and we use our computers' video cameras when we're apart. Whenever I'm picking on myself, whenever I have my attention on me and how I'm doing even to the slightest extent, she starts to place her attention on me, too and she worries about me."

"If you have your attention on yourself, you're not really on the phone call," Shya explained. "You're actually self-involved and feeling sorry for yourself and so you aren't really *there* with her."

"Since you're an actor, you could treat those phone calls as though your wife is your audience," Ariel suggested. "In the sense that, when you talk with her, you take your attention off yourself and put your attention on taking care of her. The more you can practice taking your attention off yourself, the more it will feed into every other aspect of your life. You'll be a better actor. You'll feel more fulfilled. You'll be able to see opportunities as they present themselves rather than getting lost in your thoughts."

"Your wife recently said something to me," Ariel continued. "She said, 'He doesn't like it when I go away.' Maybe you should stop fostering that, stop punishing her for leaving. As though she was your mommy."

Rod burst out laughing.

"Because her job requires that she go out of town," Shya said, "as does yours. If you punish each other for going away, it will have a negative effect on your relationship. You don't need that."

"If we do that," Rod said, "we won't allow each other to get as much work as we possibly could."

"Absolutely," Shya agreed, "because you'll be suppressing her leaving. And vice versa."

"That's great," Rod said.

HOW DO *YOU* PULL FOR ATTENTION?

Whether you're living with your partner or find yourself at a distance, our advice to Rod is something to take to heart. If you have your attention on yourself and aren't really with the person you are relating with, she (or he) feels uncertain. She'll worry if you still love her and if everything is okay between you. It doesn't free her to be fully self-expressive because her attention can either be on you and how you are doing or she can be fully engaged in her current life circumstances. She can't do both at the same time. If she is preoccupied with how you are doing, she won't be available to interact appropriately with her own life.

When we were children we got attention when we were sick, hurt, upset or in trouble. That's when people showed their love for us. Now we have learned to create problems to get attention. When we feel insecure, we revert to these childish ways of relating that do not support relationship.

We're not suggesting that you shouldn't share your concerns or talk about the challenges of your day with your partner. We are suggesting you become aware of all the ways you pull for attention. Get interested in how you automatically complain and feel sorry for yourself as an attention-getting device. These mechanisms were set in place when you were very young but they don't support having a Match Made in Heaven. As we told Rod, be kind to yourself about what you see. Kindness is key.

Distant But Connected
TransformationMadeEasy.com/matchmadeinheaven

27

SHRINK TO FIT

*O*ftentimes there comes a point in a relationship where the union is no longer expansive. Things have been said or done that were not conducive to having the relationship be harmonious. If this happens, it is time for you to communicate. It's an opportunity to look at and dissolve the mechanical behaviors that you both have learned. It is time to bring to light the things that are fettering the relationship, preventing it from growing. But all too often, being honest seems too confronting. When this occurs, you will try to monitor your actions and do your best to not make waves for fear of losing your partner. This process of self-suppression dooms the relationship to mediocrity.

If you cannot be yourself in a relationship, you no longer have one.

Rather, you are caught in a web of your own making. The way out is through completely open and honest communication—first with yourself and then with your partner.

We have often seen, particularly with women, that once they secure a relationship, they begin to whittle away at the activities they love until all that remains as the sole focus of their life energy is their boyfriend. This is never healthy. Sometimes a man will fall in love with a lively, interesting lady and then ultimately feel threatened by anything that pulls her attention away from him or makes a demand on her time. In this case, the passionate nature of the woman dims until she is but a shell of the person he first met.

In our seminars and along our travels, we occasionally come across someone who plays on their partner's insecurities in order to tie him or her more firmly to them. In this way, they feel important and more secure in themselves. These people mistakenly think that keeping your spouse's attention in this manner is a sign of "love." Here is an example of this as told from Shya's point of view.

ANYBODY'S DOG

As Ariel and I boarded a small airplane in Ft. Lauderdale bound for Eleuthera in the Bahamas, I noticed the other passengers who would be flying with us. Some seemed to be Bahamians returning from shopping trips, while others were retirees. There was a family with two small children and I enjoyed watching their young boy animate his Spiderman action figure, jumping it from his sister's shoulder, flying it from seat to seat. I also noticed a man in his mid-30s talking loudly to his wife. Dressed in casual attire, they were obviously going on vacation. Since there was only one seat on each side of the aisle, Ariel and I sat across from each other and this couple sat in front of us.

The plane prepared for take-off and I watched Ariel gaze out her window, fascinated by the view from her little portal into the world. As I turned to look out of my window, I saw that the man who had been so loud was now fidgeting in his seat while his wife did a crossword puzzle. As we sat on the tarmac before take-off, I heard him say, "Joan, this flight is going to be just like our honeymoon. Look at this plane—it's so small."

Immediately that got her attention. She anxiously said, "Do you really think so, Ted?"

"Oh yes, the ride will be exactly the same—just as rough, maybe even rougher."

She put down her pencil and grabbed his hand. I could only imagine what the airplane ride was like after they got married but this one was actually smooth and calm all the way to the island. Later, as we waited to clear customs, we chatted with them and learned that they were Joan and Ted Johnson from Seattle and that they planned to scuba dive during their vacation. Diving, he said, was a passion of his but we got the impression that he was more comfortable with the sport than she was.

A few days later, we were sitting in a restaurant at twilight. As we were watching the sun slide into the Caribbean, the Johnsons came into the restaurant and they stopped by our table to chat. Ted regaled us with tales of swimming and coming across 6-foot-long barracudas (fish with notably large teeth) and how one of them "postured aggressively." Expansively, he told us of the dangers and how he had threaded his way through the treacherous waters. It was very interesting to watch Joan in the background during his account. All the while she seemed to grow smaller and shrink into herself.

As they left our table, I suddenly remembered Laddy, a little black mutt I had when I was 14. When my neighbor, Willie White, gave me the dog, I immediately had fantasies that Laddy would be like Rin Tin Tin or Lassie, that he would be my faithful companion, following me, loving me—only me. The problem was that Laddy had an inquisitive nose, an adventurous spirit and he liked people, lots of people. Laddy wasn't just my dog, he was anybody's dog. He would happily lick anyone's face, not only mine. This bothered me in my boyish insecurity until I discovered a trick: Close to home, my dog was secure in his environment and gregarious, but when I took him to new places where he felt less secure, he would stay close by my side and look to me for comfort. When Laddy was attentive only to me, I felt needed, important and loved. But when his attention wandered I felt deflated, smaller somehow.

It was clear to me that Ted undermined Joan's sense of herself. He wanted all of her attention fixed on him and routinely played on her insecurities as a device to achieve this end.

That evening in the Bahamas, as the last red glow disappeared on the horizon, I looked at Ariel and felt happy to enjoy true love. Our relationship is not built on her loving me...only me. She loves and lives with a sense of wonder and expansiveness and I feel grateful that she chooses to share the adventure of her life with me. Undermining her sense of well-being so that she "needs" me is a child's game. Love is not something that is fostered by playing on your partner's insecurities or pulling on him or her for attention. That type of "love" is about as real and mature as an adult playing with a Spider-man action figure and believing that it actually flies.

28

HAVE YOU FORGOTTEN YOUR TRUE PRIORITIES?

After a couple has been together for a number of years, they frequently develop a routine where the day-to-day household and family duties take precedence and intimacy takes a back seat. Often they forget to rekindle the fires of passion and intimacy. They simply forget to flirt with each other and have mini-dates (and longer dates, too.) In a busy life, household duties and to-do lists become all consuming and couples begin to forget their true priorities. Here is an example in a conversation we had with our longtime friends and clients, Isabelle and Tony.

Isabelle came to us the morning we taped the video mini-sessions, complaining that she and her husband, Tony, did not make enough time for each other. There was always something that came between them. She said they had a list of things to do and those things always seemed to come first.

We sat with them in our garden as the soft fall breeze blew around us. Both in their mid- to late-40s, Isabelle is petite with short auburn hair, brown eyes and a wisp of a French accent that lingers though she has lived in the States for over 20 years. Tony is tall and athletic with thinning dark hair and strong features. He smiled at his wife as she began to speak.

"We wanted to talk to you today about the fact that we don't seem to make enough time for each other," Isabelle said. "We always have our list of things to do and it seems to always come first."

"Let me ask you a question," Shya said. "Do you ever get finished with the list of things to do?"

Isabelle quickly answered, "No."

This was an important starting point in the conversation about rediscovering intimacy with her husband because there are always going to be things that need to be done, that get added to your to-do list on a daily basis. At the end of each day, there is the high likelihood that tasks will remain. If Isabelle and Tony kept waiting until the list was complete, they would never have time for each other.

"In any healthy life," Shya explained, "there are things that need to be done that get added to your to-do list. You're going to have to put each other on your to-do list, as a priority."

It had never occurred to our friends to put themselves on their to-do lists, much less to consider their relationship itself as a priority.

It is an expansive idea to realize that your well-being and that of your partner can be as important or even more important than the tasks at hand.

Your relationship can actually take precedence. Often we get so caught up in trying to complete things or to get ahead with our life goals, we forget or disregard the health of the relationship itself.

BEING HERE WITH YOUR PARTNER

Once Isabelle and Tony caught the idea that being together could be a priority, it was time to set their to-do
list aside. While it was a great idea to schedule time for
themselves, this plan was not going to be effective if they
didn't look at one important element: Isabelle and Tony
were rarely where they were.

"What Shya said to you is true," Ariel said, "but it
doesn't matter how many times he tells you to put yourself on at the top of your to-do list, it won't be effective
unless you look at one thing:

"You may actually be in the room together but your
minds are elsewhere. You are preoccupied. You're thinking about the future and what needs to get done.

"It doesn't matter what's on your to-do list. Even if
it says to spend more time together, you'll be thinking
about how you need to spend more time with each other
while you're actually in the same room together."

Tony and Isabelle laughed in response to this, clearly
knowing the experience well. They were so habituated by
a mindset that was forward-thinking about what needed
to get done, that it didn't matter if their top priority
became "Spend more time with Tony" or "Spend more
time with Isabelle." Given their current way of being, it
was likely that when they were together they would be
thinking about the other items on their to-do lists, such
as the projects they had left to do at work.

Ariel offered them an example from our own lives to
show the depth of intimacy we experience on a daily basis, despite having been together for such a long time.

"Shya came up behind me the other day while I was
doing something," Ariel began, "and he wrapped his
arms around me and kissed the back of my neck. In all
the years we've been together this is certainly not the
first time he did that. But I was present enough to feel it.

Not that I hadn't felt it before, but in that moment I was where I was rather than distracted in my thoughts about wanting to get something done. It would've been so easy to continue with the task or to perceive his affection as an "intrusion" rather than the loving expression that it was. Had I been distracted or busy going somewhere, lost in my thoughts of what I needed to accomplish, it would have gotten between me and feeling the touch of his lips on the curve where my neck and shoulder meet, his light breath on my neck. I wouldn't have been aware of the warmth of his arms. My thoughts would have posed a barrier between him and me.

"When the two of you are with each other," Ariel continued, "you don't actually experience it because you're off in your minds going somewhere."

"So you never get fulfilled," Shya added, "because you aren't there to be fulfilled. Satisfaction and well-being happen if you're here, in this moment. If you're not in the current moment of your life, you won't experience fulfillment. Even if you're together, even if it seems as though you're in sync, if you're off thinking, there is no satisfaction as a result."

FEAR OF INTIMACY

"What keeps you thinking about different things," Shya explained, "is probably the confrontation of intimacy. There is a fear of intimacy, of just being there without a script, without knowing what to say, or knowing what to do, or knowing how to be."

"When Shya says 'intimacy,' your minds probably jumped to physical intimacy," Ariel said. "You thought he meant primarily sex. But sexual, physical intimacy is only one aspect of how you're being together. It's an extension of how you're being together in the kitchen or in the living room.

"For example," Ariel continued, "when you and the other folks were coming over to our home today to record these mini-sessions, Shya and I wanted to make a light lunch for you all. We prepared part of it last night and then part of it we did this morning. We got up quite early and were sautéing things and chopping things and mixing them all together in a big bowl. When it came time to transfer it from one container to another, Shya was holding up the bowl and I used the little spatula to scrape it. It was a very intimate moment. We had lots of things to do to prepare for everyone, but we weren't off thinking about those things that were yet to be done. We were right there with the sensuousness of scraping that bowl as Shya was holding it. I even picked that bowl to mix things in to begin with because it was so sensuous and gorgeous. We were having fun with that. If you're not there in the kitchen, when you get into bed and you're starting to be physically intimate with each other, you'll be off thinking about tomorrow morning.

"While we were preparing lunch, we were being very effective and productive as well as satisfied with ourselves and with each other. Jumping ahead in your thoughts to worry or think about something else is simply a habit. It slows down your ability to be effective and productive and it creates a barrier between you and feeling satisfied. When you're preoccupied in your thoughts, there is no intimacy.

"A lot of times when people aren't as physically intimate as they want to be," Ariel went on. "They think it's about physical intimacy, not recognizing that it starts when you get up in the morning and how you're handling your cup of coffee, tea or glass of juice."

"It's about being where you are in everything that you do," Shya said. "It's about actually being where you are rather than going somewhere in your thoughts and actions. We've discovered that when anything goes wrong around us, it's because we're rushing to get something done, so we're not there simply completing what we're doing. But if you complete things, if you're there for what you're doing, you don't make mistakes because you'll be there to do things the right way the first time.

A LITTLE TRICK: PRETEND YOU'RE SICK!

"This past spring I became sick for about a month," Ariel said. "I caught a cold when we were in Europe and it took a while for me to kick it. I just didn't have the energy to do a lot of extra things. During that time frame, I realized all of the extra things that I do rather than just being. As I've gotten my energy back, it's been an interesting game to al-low myself to still be as simple and not driving forward as I was when I didn't have the energy to do that. Interestingly enough, I get far more done now. I was actually accomplish-ing everything I needed to when I wasn't feeling well but without the extra stress and without pushing to get ahead. I know this sounds silly, but I'm going to tell you guys: Pre-tend you're sick, that you just don't have the energy to do that extra thing you want to throw in at night before going to bed. Just pretend that you don't have it in you. Just for a little bit, until you get into the habit of being."

Isabelle and Tony turned to each other, smiled, and held each other's gaze for a little while, sharing a moment of in-timacy as we sat there. Then Tony leaned forward and they kissed lightly.

"See," Ariel laughed, "it's starting already."

Isabelle and Tony turned back to us, their faces flushed with delight. "Thank you."

"Thank *you*," Shya said, grinning. "That was fun."

Your True Priorities
TransformationMadeEasy.com/matchmadeinheaven

29

BACK IN THE SADDLE AGAIN

*I*n the next section we meet Christina, a beautiful young woman in her early 30s with bright brown eyes, thick wavy chestnut hair, and an infectious smile. We know Christina well, as she is the daughter of two of our close friends and she is also our personal assistant and office manager. Over the years she's had several long-term relationships, each of which eventually ended. And yet Christina still held onto the belief that life would be better once she was in a relationship, even though her actual experience did not support this idea.

As we sat down with her in our home, she smiled broadly, clearly relaxed and happy to be sharing this moment with us. But as she began formulating her question, she reconnected with her idea about needing a relationship in order to be happy and we saw a seriousness descend upon her.

"I have a question," she began. "I feel as though I have great jobs and I'm doing well with losing weight and paying off my debts. But there's one piece missing." She looked at us, clearly a little embarrassed to admit it, "and that piece is finding a relationship."

"That's because you're trying to get a relationship," Ariel said, "rather than a date."

Christina nodded, the seriousness apparent again as she processed the answer and didn't really like it. But in the next moment the cloud passed and she began to see the truth of what Ariel had said.

"You think something is missing that will somehow fulfill you when you have it," Shya added. "This is a problem for many people. If it's not a relationship, then it's money or something else you think will fulfill you. But it will never happen. If you have a relationship, that will simply be the source of the problem next."

What Christina hadn't realized was that if you think in a problem/solution framework, once you solve your current problem, another pops up to take its place as the source of your dissatisfaction.

Listening carefully, Christina nodded in agreement. A half-smile played on her lips but a splash of seriousness lingered in her eyes. She was not ready to let go of her old beliefs just yet. No doubt she had heard us say before that a person's well-being is not determined by their circumstances. She understood and believed it intellectually. But she still held the deeply ingrained belief that a relationship would bring her happiness and that it would somehow complete and fulfill her.

"The other thing is," Ariel continued, "you're looking to fulfill a child's dream of a relationship rather than simply noticing if you're having fun dating. By the way, are you dating?"

"No," she admitted, "not now."

Ariel smiled, remembering a conversation we'd had with Christina once before when she was disappointed about dating. We had advised her to "Buy A Ticket."

BUY A TICKET

Christina came to work in our office one Saturday morning and we noticed that she seemed a bit subdued. She didn't look like her beautiful, lively self and so we sat down with her over a cup of coffee and asked if everything was all right. She began to cry and through the sniffles and tears we sorted out what seemed to be the crux of the matter. Christina was feeling lonely and wanted a boyfriend, someone whom she could spend time with, someone who would love her and touch her and be there and, yes, someone she could fall in love with—someone she could marry.

Over the course of the conversation, it became apparent that after her last relationship had dissolved, Christina had been so disappointed she'd retreated into herself. Even though she was the one to end things with her previous boyfriend, after the initial burst of energy that came from being honest and telling the truth, she felt drained, sad and unattractive.

Sitting at our dining room table, we told her a story:

There once was a man who wanted so badly to win the lottery that he complained to God on a daily basis. His complaint went something like this:

"Oh, God! Why won't you let me win the lottery? Do you hate me? I really need that money and if you were a kind God, you would have me win. If you were a fair God, surely you would support me. If you were a just God, you would make sure I have the winning numbers. Please God, let it be today."

Every day the man would sit down in his La-Z-Boy recliner and say, "God, dear God, why didn't you let me win?"

Each day the man's routine was the same. He would come home from work and complain to God that God must hate him because He had not given him the money that he so justly deserved.

One night, after going through his ritual of complaining from the comfort of his recliner, a voice suddenly came to him, pleading for help. It was large and booming and seemed to emanate from all directions at once. Thinking someone was behind him, the man quickly looked behind his chair but no one was there.

"Help me!" the voice boomed again.

Frightened now, the man jumped out of his La-Z-Boy and frantically looked around the room for the person who was calling for help but he couldn't locate the source. Finally, the man realized that the voice must be coming from heaven. Certain that his prayers had finally been heard, he fell to his knees, sure that now, with divine intervention, all of his prayers would be answered.

Once again, the voice boomed out, reverberating through the house. "Help me!" the voice entreated, "Help me! Please...buy a ticket!"

"Christina," we said, "if you want to win the lottery, you need to buy a ticket. If you want to catch a bus, you don't stand in the woods. If you want to date, you can't sit at home and expect someone who has never met you to call." We told her that if she wanted to find a boyfriend, she needed to take the actions to make it happen.

Christina was heartened by the conversation. That night she began to buy her own ticket. She joined an online dating service and when she was out, she looked around at the available men in her environment. She also stopped hiding behind her eyes, where her smile masked her disappointment and ideas of her undesirability.

One thing led to another and Christina started to participate in her own life. She found a flyer that offered training for a marathon where she could raise funds for cancer research. During her training and other activities relating to the marathon, Christina realized that she was surrounded by men, many of whom were available. Yet she still didn't regularly date. We suggested to her that she practice flirting, a smile here and there and stay present for the response. In fact, we suggested that she flirt everywhere, as she remained interested, engaged and talking to people whether it was in line at the bank or the post office or having coffee at Starbucks. It didn't matter if the person was male or female. It wasn't about getting married. When you buy a lottery ticket, you don't expect to win the pot each time. The important thing is playing the game.

Christina's chances improved each time she bought a ticket. She certainly had a much better chance of meeting a man than someone who plays the lottery and tries to win a million dollars. If you want a chance at fulfilling your dreams, you can't sit on the La-Z-Boy of life and expect God to intervene.

DOING WHAT WORKS

We'd had that conversation with Christina a few years prior and it really worked for her then. Christina had done what we suggested and she was dating again—until one of her dates led to a relationship that eventually ended. She had been so disappointed and saddened, she forgot what had initially worked. So instead of getting back into the dating saddle again, Christina did what a lot of people do when they get hurt. She stopped dating altogether.

This is very normal. When people get upset or disappointed, they forget what works. Christina had stopped buying a ticket. It was time to talk with her about what was going on.

"If you want to date," Ariel said, "you have to get started. You can't sit at home and expect that someone is going to knock on your door. If you do, it's more likely to be a Jehovah's Witness than a potential date."

We all laughed, sharing in the lightness of the moment.

"After we had that conversation with you in the past," Ariel went on, "you started successfully dating. Then you moved into a relationship that had its full life cycle and eventually ended. But then you didn't do what had worked before because you were disappointed."

"You made a decision at that point," Shya continued. "You said, 'This is too difficult, too painful. I'm not doing this again.'"

"Yes," Christina nodded, as she recalled her disappointment.

"So you contracted," Shya continued. "Decisions are always made in a moment of contraction. You never make one when you're fully expansive in yourself. You make them when things don't go the way you think you want them to. You get disappointed, you get upset, and then you make these decisions about how you're going to be in the future."

"Yes," Christina nodded. "I see that."

"That decision runs forward in time and determines how you interact with your life in the future," Shya explained, "and now you've got a couple of great jobs you enjoy doing, yet you don't feel satisfied because you think something is missing. But maybe nothing is missing."

Christina had decided to stop dating in order to avoid disappointment, but unbeknownst to her, she was stuck there. It was the First Principle of Instantaneous Transformation all over again:

What you resist, persists and dominates your life.

In Christina's bid to avoid being disappointed again, the feeling of disappointment permeated all areas of her life like a bad-smelling perfume, even the "good" areas. She was unable to fully enjoy her job and weight loss and increased financial stability or any other aspect of her life.

THE PERFECTION OF THE MOMENT

"Let's take the possibility," Shya suggested to Christina, "that this moment is absolutely perfect the way it is. In this moment you can only be right here, right now, having this conversation with us. This is a perfect moment of now, so if you're not in a relationship right now, that's perfect because you're not. But you still have the idea that in the future, something called a relationship is somehow going to fulfill you. That idea is causing you a lot of pain. Let me ask you a question." Shya sat forward. "You have had relationships. Have they been fulfilling?"

"Not really," Christina said. "No."

"You see, a relationship in and of itself is not fulfilling," Shya said. "If you're already fulfilled, however, your relationship will be very satisfying. But if you're expecting a relationship to give you a sense of well-being and satisfaction and *joie de vivre*, it's not going to happen."

"There was a time when you had the jobs you have now and you weren't feeling fulfilled," Ariel recalled, "because it's your sense of yourself that you're bringing to your life, not the other way around. The relationship is not going to fulfill you. I'm underlining what Shya just said because you thought you would be 'complete' when you get a relationship."

"Yes," Christina nodded, beginning to see her past in a whole new light. She had been attached to a false belief. Now she could see the truth that whether or not she felt fulfilled had absolutely nothing to do with her relationship status.

THERE IS NOTHING WRONG WITH YOU

"The other thing is, you are already a complete success," Ariel said. "You are successfully living out the decision you made earlier which is: 'No more of this. That did not work.' Right now you have a successful relationship with yourself. You are being true to yourself. Good job."

We all laughed and Christina nodded, her brown eyes sparkling again. "Yes," she said, understanding, "because right now I feel great."

"Yes," we replied, seeing how bright and alive she was.

"And now," Ariel said, "if you want to date, you can. It's up to you."

"But if you're going to date, Christina," Shya reminded her, "just date. Have fun with whoever you're with, wherever you are. Look, I'm being unfaithful to my wife," Shya said facetiously.

Amused, Ariel nodded.

"I'm unfaithful because I date wherever we go," Shya said.

"He's doing it right now," Ariel said, as Christina also looked amused.

"I engage with everybody I meet," Shya explained. "That's what this lifetime is about: getting involved with everyone you meet rather than looking for a Special Someone to save you. You know, the Prince is not coming. That's a fairy tale."

"So," Ariel asked, "are you having a successful date right now?"

"Yes, very much so," Christina grinned. "Thank you."

"You are very welcome," we said, enjoying the delight and excitement on Christina's face. In that moment, she had rediscovered the joys of dating.

Back in the Saddle Again
TransformationMadeEasy.com/matchmadeinheaven

30

BREAKING UP IS HARD TO DO

*O*n Wednesdays at noon Eastern Time we host our Internet radio show, *Being Here*. Over the years we have covered a wide range of topics. For one episode, we borrowed a title from a Carly Simon tune called, "These are The Good Old Days." We were surprised when our third caller, Gio, wanted to talk about his recent breakup. It was clear that in the vacuum created after his relationship ended, he had begun to forget the things that led to the dissolution of that relationship. He had started pining for the fantasy of "the good old days" when his relationship still felt good. Of course, when this happens, you don't remember things as they actually were. Your mind picks and chooses the "good" moments and forgets the rest.

Join us as we talk with our friend Gio about his breakup. Both he and his ex are in their late 20s. They are lovely people and neither was to blame. It was just one of those things where the union dissolved and it was time to move on.

"I love the topic of this show," Gio said when he called in to talk. "I've been listening and it's a really awesome show. I guess it sparked something in me and I just wanted to take this opportunity to ask about it. I had a long-term relationship end about a month ago and I've definitely been in and out of feeling sort of dim or having sad times."

"Well, let me talk with you about this, my friend," Shya said, "because I've gone through a number of breakups in my long life, including a marriage and one other time I had been engaged to be married."

"We know that your breakup was with your high school sweetheart," Ariel said.

"Right," Gio replied.

"Even though you broke up a month ago, you still have a physiological addiction to your now ex-girlfriend," Shya said.

"Yeah."

"You know, chances are you haven't recently been loved and touched and had the access to physical affection that you had when the two of you were in sync," Ariel said.

"I love how you phrased that, 'in sync,'" Shya said. "Rather than when you were living together."

"Yes, I put it that way because there were times, especially toward the end, where it was combative, so there was no nurturing in that," Ariel said. "But what is happening now, Gio, is that you're having withdrawals."

"Yes," Shya said. "You're in withdrawal from your addiction, that's all. I remember when I got a divorce. I worked at that time for a company where we counseled people, so I sought counseling from one my advisors. I can't remember who he was at this point because it was a long time ago, something like 35 years, but he said something to the effect of, 'You know, you'll think about your ex-wife 24 hours a day for the first week that you break up. The second week, you'll only think about her all of your waking hours and then the week after that about 8 hours a day. A couple of months down the road, maybe you'll think about her 3 or 4 hours a day, and then if you're lucky, a year later, you won't think about her at all.'"

Gio laughed. He recognized himself in Shya's story.

"That's the way it is with addictions," Shya said.

"Yes, wow," Gio said. He could see it all laid out in front of him—the times he felt dim and lost and having "sad times" were usually late at night when he was dreaming of what once was... or at least his fantasy of how it once had been.

"I imagine you're on a faster timeline than the one Shya just described." Ariel said, "because I've seen you in the last month and there were moments where I saw you really come out through your eyes and really be here. When I say 'come out through your eyes,' I mean, come out of the dim zone."

"Yes," Shya said. "This is when you're not lost in your thoughts."

"Yeah, it's true," Gio said.

"Part of why you get lost in your thoughts and are sad is when you wish things were different as if this isn't your choice." Ariel said.

"In those moments," Shya said, "you remember those days in the relationship as 'the good old days.' You wonder if you should have done something to save it or think about if you should have stayed together and you worry about if you could have said something or done something different."

"Yeah, I do that," Gio said.

"I know you guys broke up in the past and then you got back together again for a while," Ariel said. "But there were certain mechanics between the two of you that did not want to be brought to light and dissolved. Being together was not more important than letting go of those mechanics. You mentioned something to me a while ago about feeling like you had to drag her into life sometimes. I'm sure if I sat down with her, she would have things to tell me about what she felt you didn't do and those things that you wouldn't let go. Shya and I each had really strong mechanics as well, but for whatever reason, being with each other was more important than hanging on to those old familiar ways of relating. And really, Gio, you've been feeling sorry for yourself as if this breakup was not your idea."

"Even though you initiated it." Shya said.

"Yup. That's right," Gio said.

"I would suggest that you become the author of your life and your life choices rather than the victim." Shya said.

"Cool. I like it." Gio said.

"Yeah, really. You know, you chose to break up with your ex-girlfriend, well fine, then move on," Shya said.

Gio chuckled quietly in the background.

Suddenly Shya had an epiphany. "Oh, Gio, I got it," Shya said as if a light bulb had just lit up with the answer as to why Gio had been in mourning for his ex. "You're Catholic, aren't you?"

"Yes," Gio replied.

"You think that you need to do penance now because your relationship ended."

Gio started laughing. Shya had pulled a thread of his enculturation and he was unraveling the web that kept Gio's misery in place.

"In your mind, it was a marriage of sorts and basically you're getting a divorce from that point of view," Shya said.

"Yeah," Gio agreed.

"Can you get an annulment?" Ariel asked, "Can we give you absolution somehow?"

Gio laughed again as we made light of the situation. He was lightening up as well.

"Maybe we can have him do some *Our Fathers* or *Hail Marys* and that might be enough," Shya suggested.

"That's so funny," Gio said. "That really is what it has felt like!"

"I actually think both of you should celebrate," said Ariel. "You're both so lovely—both of you. You don't have to split up your friends and divide who's Gio's friend and who's her friend. You don't have to have this be some big, awful, emotional time in your lives."

"Yeah, it doesn't have to be acrimonious," Shya said.

"Yeah, cool," Gio said. You could almost see him nodding as the idea of having it be easy fell into place. "I'm into that. I like it. Yeah."

"Good," Ariel said.

"Yeah," Gio replied.

"Gio, be kind to yourself," Shya suggested. "Stop beating on yourself for going for your life and going for your truth."

"I'll tell you something. Right now it's a challenge because you are likely to think, 'Oh, will I ever find someone?'" Ariel said.

Shya continued. "When a relationship breaks up, both parties are desirous of it. Both parties are done with that relationship, but one has the courage to say, 'This isn't working, I'm out of here.' That person usually takes the heat or the blame for the breakup."

"Give yourself a break, give her a break, and enjoy your life. This is the moment," Ariel said.

"This is it," Shya said. "*This* is the good old moment."

"Oh, I love you guys! Thank you," Gio said.

"Well thank you for loving us. We love you too, Gio," Shya replied.

"We love you, too—dearly. We love her dearly, too!" Ariel said.

"Yeah." Shya confirmed.

The conversation came to the end at the perfect moment. Ariel closed out the show with our usual tagline:

"We have to go. We'll be back next week. Come on back everyone and don't miss *Being Here.*"

As we hung up the phone, we were happy for Gio and for his ex-girlfriend. When most people break up, they have very challenging months or even years. Friends take sides. One group is loyal to one party and agrees to dislike the other. But we have been witness to another possibility: A Transformational Approach to Dating, Relating and Marriage. This includes a transformational approach to breakups as well.

These are the Good Old Days:
Breaking Up is Hard to Do
TransformationMadeEasy.com/matchmadeinheaven

31

TIME ON THE WATER:
AN ANGLER'S GUIDE TO DATING

*O*ne day, Shya and I went fishing on the Delaware River. It was late afternoon as we launched our little aluminum boat, the slanting sunlight dancing on the water. Two days prior, while taking a walk, we had stood on the bridge that crossed this section of the Delaware and had spied many fish: bass, crappies and bluegills. The fish were all holding in one small pool between an island and the western edge and we were looking forward to motoring over to that area and trying out some of Shya's flies to see what we could catch.

The recent spring rains had raised the water level, creating an island between the main river and what was now a small channel of water. In summer, this little waterway is too shallow to navigate but for now it was perfect for drifting and casting to either side.

At first we cast little green and orange buggy-looking things with "silly legs," little strips of rubber that would undulate with the water's movement, looking like a bug in distress. This type of fly is called a "popper." With a quick strip of the line, you pull the popper through the water, making a splash and a plopping sound in a bid to attract the nearby fish.

As we floated along, Shya set up our electric motor

on the front of the boat so if we got too close to either shore we could gently and quietly reposition ourselves in a more advantageous spot for fishing. We could see submerged rocks and logs and all sorts of structure that fish normally like to hide behind, areas where they feel safe. Cast after cast we made into this nook and that cranny and yet we had very little response from fish, so we decided it was time for a change.

By now we had floated down the channel until we were in position to cast to the pool we had viewed from the bridge. Throwing the anchor overboard, we laughed at the noise as the chain clanked along the side of the aluminum boat as we prepared to anchor up. Shya turned to me with a grin. "Stealth," he said poking fun at himself, "that's called stealth."

Over the years we've learned that it's always best to be as quiet as possible in order to not alert the fish to your presence, in order to not scare them off. However, bass, bluegills and crappies are not the most skittish of fish, so we knew we would be fine.

As the boat settled into the stream, we switched flies, putting on a Goddard caddis fly. This type of fly is made with deer hair and feathers and does a pretty good job of imitating an aquatic insect called a caddis fly. (Goddard was the fellow who originated this particular pattern.) Before we knew it, we were hooking and releasing some beautiful little fish. We were in the right location, using an attractive fly, with the skills needed to make a delicate presentation and the presence needed to set the hook when the fish took the bite.

Side by side we fished. (Or perhaps I should say back-to-back, since I was in the bow, or the front, of the boat and Shya was in the stern.) We were there for some time, the light playing off the water, the birds singing, the occasional car or pedestrian passing by on the bridge overhead, the snow geese bathing near the shore.

At one point a fish splashed by my caddis as it tried to grab it for dinner. With a quick jerk I raised the rod to set the hook. I missed the fish and the fly came hurtling out of the water, wrapping itself around the engine and various other things that were catchable in the bottom of the boat. When I unwrapped the line from around the motor, I found that the tippet of my line and the fly itself were all bollixed up in a tangled mess.

As I sat down to work out the mess, I came to a startling realization: We had been on the river for a couple of hours now and this was the first time I'd had a snarl. It wasn't something I did by casting incorrectly. It was the result of snapping the line back without the weight of a fish to stop its trajectory back into our boat. Once again, I had underestimated my skill with fishing. And yet I have not always been so skilled. I still carry with me the memory of my learning curve, which was steep and often frustrating. Yet by simply getting back out there again and again, I had learned and grown so organically, I hadn't even noticed how I had moved from novice through amateur to expert.

There is an old saying, "Time on the Water." There were plenty of times when Shya and I have gone fishing and we didn't catch a thing, so we just chalked it up to experience and time on the water. It is said that when an angler wants to improve, there is no substitute for time on the water. When we haven't caught something—well, that's why they call the sport "fishing," not "catching."

Patiently, I worked out the puzzle before me, unweaving the tangled, snarled line. I have learned over many years of fishing that if I become frustrated and express my impatience by tugging on the knot, it only tightens the mess. But calmly unwinding what has been woven by accident is the fastest way to get it untangled.

As my fingers worked, my mind drifted. I suddenly realized how in the early days, as much as I found having a rat's nest at the end of my line inconvenient, it was also somehow a relief. While I was working on a problem in my line that prevented me from fishing, I didn't have the pressure of trying to make a cast when I wasn't very skilled. I didn't have to feel like a failure if I couldn't make a decent presentation. I didn't have to feel "rejected" by fish when I put out cast after cast without having so much as a bite. I didn't have to compare myself to Shya or to other people whom I felt were better at it than I was. In other words, this problem with my line used to be a chance to back off and rest. It was certainly less confrontational than fishing.

As I finally unsnarled my tangled lines, a thought came swimming up from deep within. I suddenly flashed on my friends who are still dating. "Fishing is a lot like dating," I thought. Sometimes having a problem with something can be a relief. When working on a problem that prevents people from dating, they don't have the pressure of trying to make a date when they aren't skilled as yet. They don't have to feel like a failure if they think they aren't presentable. When diverted by sorting out a problem, they don't have to feel rejected when they put out cast after cast without having so much as a bite. And they don't have to compare themselves to Shya or me or any of the other people whom they feel are better at relating than they are. In other words, this problem with their lives can be used as a chance to back off and rest. It is certainly less confrontational than fishing...or should I say dating.

Oftentimes folks are frustrated that they haven't found "The One." I guess that's why it is called dating, not marriage. There is no substitute for time on the water.

"Hmm," I thought as I straightened my line, stood up and began casting again.

32

DATING AFTER DIVORCE

Sometimes people come to us with a problem or a question but they're looking in the wrong place for answers. When they direct their attention to what is really going on, their "problems" are easy to solve.

Such was the case with Kat, a petite young woman who has straight brown hair that falls past her shoulders and a captivating smile. When we sat down with her, Kat had been legally separated from her husband for nearly a year. In the state of New York where she resides, the law requires that couples wishing to divorce wait for a one-year period before initiating the final divorce proceedings. During this waiting period, Kat had begun dating.

"There's a guy that I really, really like," Kat enthused. "We've been on a few dates but he doesn't feel the same way about me."

"Forget him," Ariel said, jumping right into the conversation.

"That's exactly what I was going to say," Shya said. "Find another guy. You live in New York City. You probably have a hundred thousand excellent prospects—just on your block!" Shya added jokingly. "Aside from that, you are a beautiful woman."

We have often met people who fixate on one disinter-
ested party to the exclusion of all others. It's as if the whole
world of potential candidates for dating and relationship
ceases to exist while standing in the shadow of that one
fantasy "someone." Obviously, if Kat had been thinking
with a clearer head, she wouldn't really want someone
who didn't find her attractive or desirable...or would she?
Perhaps unrequited attraction fit the bill quite nicely.

"He's convenient," Ariel said. "Where are you currently
in your divorce proceedings? When will that become a reality?"

Kat became serious. "I can file for divorce in a few
months and then I think it takes a few months after that
before everything is finalized."

"Then this new guy is very convenient," Ariel smiled.

"How so?" Kat asked leaning forward.

"Because you are honorable," Ariel explained. "Even
though you and your ex have been separated for some
time, you once exchanged wedding vows with him which
have not yet been legally dissolved. On some level there is
a part of you that is maneuvering to remain honorable to
those vows. Which means that somebody who has no interest in you rather than somebody who is your life mate,
is really convenient at this time."

"Oh my goodness, I didn't see that," Kat said, clearly
delighted. "That is very cool."

"The other thing is, you have issues around intimacy,"
Shya said. "You won't have to deal with them with someone who doesn't want to be with you. You focus on the re-
jection and wonder, 'What's wrong with me that he doesn't
want to be with me?' rather than, 'What if we get intimate
and I have to deal with my inhibitions?'"

"Yes," Kat nodded. "That's right."

"You can come forward," Ariel continued, "and he isn't
going to reciprocate. But what about when you come for-

ward and the person turns his full interest on you?"

As she spoke, Ariel turned away from Kat and then turned back, eyes wide and smiling, bringing her attention completely to Kat.

"Well," Kat replied, noticeably uncomfortable, "that usually freaks me out."

"It freaks you out when I do it, and we aren't even dating," Ariel said as we all laughed.

"This man that you 'really, really like' currently fills a whole number of wonderful avoidance mechanisms."

"That is very cool," Kat said, "because I've often wondered why I am so interested in not only this guy, but other people who aren't available."

"Because that way you have no commitment," Shya said.

"It's not a problem then," Ariel added, "it's a solution. You may as well enjoy it. Instead of looking for another person to have a relationship with, maybe you should just have fun dating."

"Yes," Shya agreed. But as he began speaking, Kat didn't turn to look at him. Rather, she kept her attention focused on Ariel, even though Ariel had clearly finished her sentence and had already made her point.

"Ahh," Shya said. "That's very interesting. I notice that it took you a while to look at me when I started speaking. You still have stuff going on with men, Kat. You don't want to be dominated by them or told what to do—not even to have your attention requested in an interaction. When I started speaking I was an intrusion. You were having a conversation with your girlfriend. Now, unless you want a love relationship with a girl, you need to include men when they speak to you."

This was really good information for Kat as she began her dating life anew. Many times, particularly if your previous relationship was combative or if you are carrying around incompletions with your dad, you will be less than responsive to a man as he talks to you. It was as if even simple conversations had to get through a maze while Kat was busy proving to herself that she was not being dominated.

You might wonder if "not wanting to be told what to do" contributed to Kat's marriage ending in the first place. Perhaps. But that wasn't relevant at that moment. However, if Kat ultimately wanted a Match Made in Heaven, she needed to discover how to include men and listen to them rather than automatically resist them.

"Start to pay attention to how guarded you are, Kat," said Shya. "You don't have to be afraid that this conversation is leading anywhere, like a date where you might have to confront being intimate. I'm safe because I'm not trying to strike up a romantic relationship with you. I don't need a date." Shya smiled and playfully nudged Ariel. "I've got this one."

Kat flashed us a smile as she relaxed even further. It might have been easy to miss her guarded nature initially because she has such a ready smile and is so personable and attractive.

"This is a really good time frame for you to practice being intimate," Ariel said. "I know one of your jobs is being a waitress. One thing you can do, whether your customers are couples or singles, is to actually connect with them. Just keep practicing connection. When you go to Starbucks and order a coffee, connect. Then it won't be as much of a challenge when you're ready and free to actually fully connect with someone romantically again."

"Oh," Kat said, "that's wonderful. Thank you."

"You are very welcome," we said.

It's Not a Problem, It's a Solution
TransformationMadeEasy.com/matchmadeinheaven

33

THE PROPER CARE AND FEEDING OF TRACY

*I*n this chapter we meet Tracy, an attractive woman in her early 30s with springy auburn curls, creamy skin and rosy cheeks. We sat down in our garden on a crisp spring day and Tracy told us what she thought was the problem.

"I have been noticing, both at work and outside of work, that I feel anxious or nervous around certain people," Tracy stumbled on her words. "I might try to avoid them by not going to the kitchen or bathroom if they are there."

"Okay," Shya said. "So, it's not all people—it's certain people."

"Yes."

"Are these people men or women?"

She paused to consider. "I think it's mostly men."

"Good. Now, what precisely happens?"

"Do you mean how do I feel?"

"Yes. What happens in you?"

"I get tight in my chest," Tracy explained.

"Is it the same body sensations with all these people," Shya asked, "or do you get different body sensations depending on the person?"

Tracy paused again. "I'm not really sure."

When Shya suggested she take a look, she said that she felt different, depending on the person.

"I have another question about this," Ariel said, "particularly because you said that most of these people you feel anxious around are men. It makes me wonder if you are well fed."

Tracy's eyes grew wide, as if she were startled.

"What I mean by that," Ariel explained, "is if a person isn't fed physically, in other words hasn't had enough physical intimacy, sometimes when another person comes near them, their need to be loved and touched gets revved up. It's really inconvenient if the person who walks by is in a relationship, or is your boss. But your body doesn't care, it's just looking for 'food.'"

"Okay," Tracy laughed as she caught the idea. "That's right."

"I'm wondering if you're well fed. Are you in a relationship?"

"Yes, but I'm not well fed at the moment," Tracy chuckled. It was sweet to see her looking at this subject with humor.

"Are you fighting in that relationship?" Shya asked.

"Yes, but it's much better now than it has been, so I think I'll be fed soon."

"Well, who is it up to?" Shya asked.

"The proper care and feeding of Tracy is up to who?" Ariel prompted.

"Me," Tracy acknowledged with a smile. "Me."

WITHHOLDING SEX

"If you haven't been well fed, you've been withholding yourself or trying to be right about something," Ariel explained. "Because, as is the case in most relationships, if you were to make your interests known, most men will comply. If you aren't being well fed enough in the intimacy department, you shut things down. You're the one who has said 'no.'"

"Yes," Tracy said, looking soft and vulnerable. "I do feel shut down in that department."

"Well, once you notice that the door has swung shut, you can open it back up," Ariel said. "But it'll take giving up being right. Because when you're right, you're going to punish him. But the person you're really punishing is you."

"You'll punish him by withholding pleasure for yourself," Shya said.

"Yes," she said rather automatically but then her breath hitched as she caught the true meaning of Shya's words. "You mean by giving him the satisfaction of pleasuring me?" Tracy asked.

"That's right," Shya said. "Because if you have pleasure then he'll have pleasure. If you're fighting, then you certainly don't want him to have any pleasure."

"Yeah, right," Tracy said nodding, grimacing slightly, "I'm holding him hostage for something."

"What did he do or not do?" Shya asked.

"He strayed for a while."

"And what was your part in his straying?" Shya asked.

Tracy bit her lip, her eyes welled with tears. We were well aware that Tracy wasn't to "blame" for her partner's infidelity. But if Tracy looked at things as if she were 100% responsible for the health of her relationship, she would be able to extricate herself from feeling like a victim. Each person brings mechanical ways of relating into a relationship. If Tracy could identify how she had been operating with her boyfriend, without judging herself (or him) for what she saw, then perhaps they would still have a chance.

"Do you have any idea about your part?" Ariel prompted but Tracy remained mute as she choked back the emotions.

"Were you withholding before he strayed?"

Tracy nodded, tears in her eyes.

"He was hungry," Ariel explained.

"That was what caused the straying. You see, a hungry dog leaves home but a well-fed dog stays at home. Not to call him a dog, of course." Shya said, lightening the mood. "But the reality is that if you are well fed at home you don't have to stray."

"Yes, I know."

"One thing you want to be sure of, particularly now that you have no longer been monogamous at this point, is to get tested. You both should be tested for HIV and other sexually transmitted diseases," Ariel said.

"Yeah, I did ask him so he's supposed to go."

"But what about you?" Shya asked. "Have you been using condoms since you got back together?"

"We haven't had sex since we got back together."

"Then another thing you really should take a look at is whether or not you are done with him," Ariel said. "Because if you're done with him, it's time to move on. For some people, if their partner strays, then that's it. The relationship is over. Others may be interested in looking at the dynamics that set up the straying. Perhaps you have enough of a connection with him that you're willing to give it a try again under different ground rules. But you have to look at what is true for you. Because you're going to be unhappy if you're really done with the relationship but you try to keep it going.

"If, however, it's not actually that much of a big deal to you, because it's possible that it isn't, then you may be punishing him because you think it should be."

"Yes," Tracy considered. "I think that sometimes. But I've told some of my friends and they think I should leave him."

"Oh, that can complicate things."

By now the tone of the conversation had turned light again and Tracy's rosy complexion had returned. We realized that some of what she had been wrestling with was her friends' current opinions about her boyfriend. Well-meaning friends will take our side in a dispute but rarely will they stop to see that a relationship is a dynamic between two people. Tracy may have room in her heart to forgive her boyfriend's transgression but the conflict could still be fueled by her friends' points of view.

"How long ago did this event happen?" Ariel asked.

"About three months ago."

"Oh!" Ariel said with a smile, "You haven't had food in three months?"

"Well, yes," Tracy laughed, "except with myself."

"But with yourself is energetically very different than with your partner," Ariel said. "That's like having rice everyday. Only rice. It gets boring after a while."

"Yes," Tracy said with a smile. "And I've been starting to fantasize about other people."

"How often do you see this guy at the moment?" Ariel asked.

"We live together," Tracy said.

"So it's a war zone," Shya said. "Do you sleep in the same bed?"

Tracy nodded.

"If you are so at war with each other, because this is a mutual fight, that you'll sleep in the same bed and withhold sex and love and intimacy to punish each other without bringing it to resolution, I don't know that this relationship will ever be truly satisfying."

Shya added, "Unless you're sadistic or masochistic and need to punish and be punished."

"I hope not," Tracy said.

"Or if you aren't easy with intimacy," Ariel suggested, "this event makes it easy to avoid that. I'm not only talking about physical intimacy but emotional intimacy too. Or this may fulfill some other story. For example, if you think that you are broken or there is something wrong with you then the situation as it stands proves that story right."

ACKNOWLEDGING AND ACTING ON YOUR TRUTH

"I have another question," Ariel said. "If you were not living with this man, if it were not complex, would you still be dating him?"

"I don't know," Tracy said, biting her lip. "I've asked myself that question, but I don't know."

"I don't think that's true," Ariel said. "I think you do know but your answer is inconvenient. Now, the answer may not be static. But if you look right now, you have a truth in this moment. Yet you aren't willing to say it because you're afraid that over time it's going to mean something."

"Yes," Shya continued. "You're afraid that if you look and tell the truth, it means you'll have to do something in the future rather than just look and see what's true for you. It's actually easier for you to seem confused than to look and say, 'Yes, I would still be dating him' or 'No, I would definitely be on to someone else.'"

Tracy sat in silence for a while, contemplating our words, nodding her head, a slight smile playing about her lips, her sweetness apparent.

"You are very attractive," Ariel said. "It's a shame for you to waste your bloom time locked in a battle. There is another possibility. I would really get interested in the proper care and feeding of Tracy."

"Okay," Tracy mused. "Okay."

As she pondered our words, we weren't sure whether or not she would act upon our suggestions. It was clear that she resonated with what we had said but that didn't mean she was ready to be honest with herself and find the courage to act on her truth, whatever that may be. We would have to wait and see.

Six months later, we discovered that Tracy's situation had remained much the same. Although her boyfriend had been tested for sexually transmitted diseases, they still had not shared physical intimacy. We don't know for sure why Tracy, who was clearly so lovely and desirable (at least to us), would live in this manner for such a protracted amount of time. Obviously, she didn't see herself as we saw her.

Without a doubt there was a benefit in continuing the status quo. It certainly relieved the pressure of moving past her inhibitions. She didn't have to face the daunting world of finding a new place to live nor beginning to date anew. Perhaps her parents disapproved of this fellow and to let him go would have been an admission that they were right. Or perhaps she thought this relationship was the only thing saving her from being alone or having to go back home and take care of her aging parents. Any and all of these are reason enough to stay paralyzed and indecisive if you need a good reason. But one thing is for sure, Tracy hadn't yet learned how to surrender to fully being with another.

Perhaps after all is said and done, Tracy kept the situation frozen in place so that she wouldn't have to face her own prudish nature, for living in a sexless union allowed her to avoid it.

The Proper Care and Feeding of Tracy
TransformationMadeEasy.com/matchmadeinheaven

34

YOUR PRUDISH NATURE

*I*n this chapter we meet Adam, a teenager who had just begun the dating process. At age 19, he had grown a beard, perhaps in a bid to disguise his youth and lack of experience. What most young people don't realize is that lack of experience can be a gift if you embrace it. Oftentimes they try to be more worldly than they are and adopt a guarded "I already know that" stance that follows them into physically intimate situations. When this is the case, early sexual encounters are no longer an opportunity for wonder and exploration. Instead, they are often furtive gropings in the dark. Sometimes they are fueled by alcohol as a means to bypass inhibitions and override gaps in knowledge.

Even if you are a "mature" reader with years of sexual experience and a well-established relationship behind you, as you read this section, keep in mind that your approach to sexual intimacy was set in place at a much younger age than Adam's. If you pay attention, you may just see yourself in him and discover unplumbed depths in your ability to be intimate. You may also find yourself refreshed with the newness of youthful inexperience.

BEING INTIMATE

Adam is an attractive young man, slightly stocky with short auburn hair. Sporting thick dark-rimmed glasses, a deep blue shirt and a slightly nervous demeanor, Adam began by laying out his "problem" with intimacy.

"I find I get uncomfortable with in...intimacy," he stumbled, clearly judging himself for this particular "failing."

"Well, I don't know anyone who is comfortable with intimacy." Shya said putting Adam's problem in perspective. "So you're in the right place."

Everyone laughed. Relief spread across Adam's face as he realized there wasn't anything wrong with him. "Okay," he said.

"You think that your discomfort with intimacy has to do with your experience or lack of experience, your age or your youth," Ariel explained. "You have a set of circumstances that you think are the cause. But actually discomfort with intimacy is nearly universal."

"There's a discomfort that people have in just being," Shya went on. "It's much easier if you have something to do, a script to operate from. But the idea of just being with another person is disturbing because it rattles whatever inhibitions you have. At age 19 you naturally have disturbance in you. More so than at other times, due to all the hormones influencing you."

"Yes," Adam said, nodding.

"The trick with intimacy is to relax," Shya explained. "Rather than doing something to get away from those feelings, allow yourself to feel what you're feeling. That's really the bottom line."

Ariel added, "Many people blame their circumstances for the way they feel. If they're on a date and feel nervous, or if they're naked in bed with a new lover, they believe it's the situation that causes the discomfort. But these feelings were already within them just waiting to surface."

OUR PRUDISH NATURES

Adam had arrived that day in a shirt that didn't look good on camera so someone had offered to loan him one. As Adam changed his shirt it was obvious that he was worried about his physique, expecting others to judge him the way he judged himself. He was not only embarrassed to be seen, but he was also embarrassed about his shyness. He hadn't yet realized that most of us grew up in societies that viewed the naked body and sex as taboo. When we were very young, each of us initially explored our nakedness with uninhibited delight. But this was trained out of us quite quickly.

"Another thing that is fairly universal is your prudish nature," Ariel explained. "You have inhibitions and discomfort around your body. For example, you were changing your shirt earlier and it was almost intolerable for you to be seen."

"Yes," Adam nodded.

"On a beach, going without a shirt and letting people see your naked upper body would be okay," Ariel continued, "because there are enough people there that you hope nobody is looking. Also the ground rules for the beach are that you can wear fewer clothes than you normally would and it's okay. But imagine what would happen if we were all having dinner in a restaurant in our bathing suits. If this were the case, everybody would be thinking, 'Where do I look? How do I act?' Social convention can sometimes bypass your discomfort but the discomfort is still there."

Adam began to feel more relaxed about himself in general and more specifically about the topic of conversation.

"It's not just with you, Adam," Ariel explained. "In general, people feel uncomfortable around their bodies and bodily functions. We learn it. It comes along with the enculturation. Some people don't have a lot of inhibitions but most do. You shouldn't feel embarrassed for being self-conscious. It's normal. You just need to find somebody to play with."

BEING COMFORTABLE WITH YOURSELF

"Yes," Shya agreed, "that's true too. But let's go back to you for a second. It's about getting comfortable with you first. If you're comfortable with yourself then intimacy becomes much easier. But if you're uncomfortable with you, you think the other person will be, too. The trick is to discover that you can't be different than you are in the current moment. So you might as well enjoy what you're feeling.

"For example, Adam, do you know those body sensations you get when there's a possibility of intimacy?"

"Yes," Adam said.

"Start enjoying them volitionally. I know it's not what you would prefer. But make it what you would prefer, because that's what is showing up. Just play a game with yourself where you trick yourself into allowing what is to be the way it is rather than wishing it were different. Incidentally, if you let yourself feel what you're feeling, then when you do have sex, it will be more pleasurable because you are there to feel it!"

"I see that," Adam said as he settled into the intimacy of being with us. It was a pleasure to see how he had become comfortable with just being. That moment was very intimate.

"Thank you," he said.

"You're welcome," we replied.

UNSTATED BUT KNOWN

Many of your inhibitions were absorbed from the culture you were surrounded by. Here is an example from Ariel's childhood:

One of my earliest memories is playing in the yard with my friend, Stevie Emerick. I must have been around age five because he and I attended the same kindergarten and he moved away shortly thereafter. At the time, Stevie was one of my best friends. It was a hot day and we were playing in our underwear, running through the sprinkler that was watering the lawn—me in my Buster Brown's and he in his briefs. Some of my parents' friends came over for a visit and frantically I looked for a shirt. I wanted to cover up. My mom began to laugh. She wasn't being unkind; she just thought it was rather silly. She said, "Ariel, you don't need a shirt." But I did. In my mind I did. I was ashamed of the two small dots of brown on my chest. They looked no different than those on Stevie's chest but somehow I knew it was shameful to let my nipples be seen. Before I attended grade school, I had already become aware of the idea that parts of my body were embarrassing and needed to be hidden.

We have all internalized ideas about our bodies from our environments. They are not bad or good—they just are.

With awareness you can dissolve the inhibitions that act as barriers between you and yourself and you and your partner. With practice you can discover, once again, a childlike innocence and the ability to feel well in your own skin.

Intimacy and Your Prudish Nature
TransformationMadeEasy.com/matchmadeinheaven

35

INTIMACY: BEING AT HOME WITH YOURSELF

*M*any people reading this book will believe that since you have had more sexual experience than Adam has had, you are more at ease in your body than he was. But is this really true? Even if it is, what if there are still unknowns, hidden pieces to you—things about your body that you have overlooked, never seen or have just plain flat out judged?

From time to time the two of us have taught courses in intimacy and sexuality and there is an assignment that we sometimes offer to participants in the course. Perhaps you would like to try it.

Here it is:

We suggest that you find a room with a full-length mirror—preferably a room that is well lit, and arrange a time that will be free from interruptions. If you don't have one already, get yourself a hand mirror, the larger the better. They are easy to find at your local beauty supply, drugstore or Walmart. You will also need a timer—a kitchen timer or an alarm on your phone will work quite nicely for this project. Now, be prepared for a truly anthropological experiment, one where your nonjudgmental nature is employed and your prejudices are set aside in order to see—really see.

The game is to get totally naked and stand in front of the mirror in your well-lit room with your hand mirror ready and your alarm set for a minimum of 15 minutes. 30 is preferable. Once you start your timer, hide its face so you will not be distracted by time but will have the opportunity to lose yourself in the exercise.

Are you hyperventilating at the simple thought of standing naked, preparing to actually look in the mirror? Have you already decided that there is absolutely no way you are going to try this? If so, you are securely locked inside a judgment system that will not lead to intimacy with yourself—or with your partner or potential partner.

Let's finish the instructions for this experiment for those who are interested:

The game is to pretend you are an alien, one who has never seen a body and has no preconceived notion of good parts and bad, pretty or ugly, old and young, shapely or shapeless.

1. Simply look, observe, see how your body is connected.
2. Look at the colors, the shapes, the textures, and observe where there is hair and where there is none.
3. Feel free to get on the floor and open your legs and actually see what is there. Or get on your hands and knees and use your hand mirror to see yourself from all different angles.

This exercise is not for the purpose of getting anywhere or for turning yourself on or for anything other than actually looking at your body without judging what you see. If you really do this, you will not be talking to yourself about wrinkles or zits or how hairy your genitals are. You will be seeing a line, or the difference in texture and color at your nipples, labia or scrotum. If you really let go, you won't pick yourself apart, thinking, "I'm fat" or "My feet are unattractive," for instance. Those are concepts that have been enculturated into you along with ideas about beauty. Rather, look at your body as though you are an alien who is suddenly inhabiting this organic housing, becoming intimately familiar with all of its parts.

Sometimes when engaging in this exercise, people have seen parts of themselves that they didn't know existed. Or they have seen an area of the body that they have never looked at before.

Go ahead—stare! We know you have been taught that it is rude to stare but don't forget, you are an alien now. Touch a nipple with a finger, for instance and see how the skin responds. Look inside your labia or pull back the foreskin if you are not circumcised. Look. See. Feel. Touch. Smell. Experience.

Again, this is not an exercise in sexuality. It is an exercise in being with your body without judgment.

AN EXERCISE IN BEING

A woman named Sue attended one of our workshops where we had given this very assignment. The next day, the participants talked about the experience and Sue revealed that during her half hour exploration she began to masturbate and subsequently masturbated until she reached an orgasm. As we talked about it, she came to realize that touching herself in this manner during the exercise, while not having been a "bad" thing to do, was actually an escape. She began to recognize that she had lots of inhibitions and had found looking at herself very confronting.

Masturbating for Sue was a way to go to the known, stop looking and in effect close her eyes. As we talked with her, Sue realized that she had, in truth, avoided the exercise. Grasping the concept that there was really nothing to be fearful of, she went back to her hotel over lunch and actually did the assignment.

Sue returned from lunch that day truly excited—and we don't mean sexually. She reported that she had always hated to look at her face. In her youth, Sue's sisters had teased her mercilessly about the freckles on her nose and she avoided looking at them and the freckles on her arms as well. She hardly even thought of them as ugly any more. She simply avoided looking at them altogether. But this time Sue looked at her freckles, really looked. And they weren't ugly or beautiful. They simply were. She looked at the broad expanse of skin on her back, noticed blemishes without picking on them (literally and figuratively) and she explored her genitals in a more clinical or detached manner, too. Sue realized that she had never really seen her clitoris. Nor had she seen the play of colors and textures in and around her genital region.

As Sue unabashedly shared with the group what she had discovered about her body, it became apparent that although she was married, she was still carrying a lot of inhibitions with her. In fact, she discovered that just as she initially had masturbated to avoid the assignment the first time, she often used sex to mask how prudish she really was.

We have often met people who assumed that because they had many partners over the years or because they'd been married for a long time, there was no prudishness left in them. In fact, they viewed being "prudish" as a failing or un-cool or something to assign to one's parents but not to oneself. By judging someone who has sexual "hang-ups" as bad, they turn a blind eye to their personal pockets of discomfort that are waiting to be discovered and experienced.

36

BIRTH CONTROL
AND INTIMACY

*I*t was a bright spring day when we sat down with our friends, Caitlin and Rod. The trees and lawn behind them were a vibrant green, birds were singing, a light breeze was blowing. Although they were more than willing to talk about their sex life and birth control, it was still a bit challenging for them. As Rod launched into the subject, his words came out a little discombobulated—in fits and starts.

"You know we went through a little... challenge," Rod said, glancing at his wife. "...Something new in our relationship." Collecting his thoughts and taking a breath, he continued in earnest, "I'll just talk about it. You know, we decided to go off birth control and so..."

"No," Caitlin gently corrected him, "Off the pill."

"Off the pill, sorry. Not off birth control," he said chuckling. "I meant we decided to get off the pill for health reasons. And, you know, we were trying to navigate how, after having sex without using condoms for such a long time, how to—what the next step was. So, I think, we went through a period where we weren't having as much sex."

"Yeah, that's right," Caitlin confirmed, nodding, now that he got it straight.

"But..." he said meaningfully with a trace of a grin. That single word was very potent. You could see that he was amused yet dismayed by this turn of events. Caitlin's no longer taking a contraceptive pill was creating complications that neither of them had anticipated.

"Well," Ariel laughed, "that's one way to navigate not getting pregnant—by not having any sex."

"Yes," Rod said, "that wasn't the best option."

"There were definitely things that came up about having sex," Caitlin continued. "Like it wasn't as easy. It wasn't as..." and now she, too, found herself at a loss for words.

"Spontaneous," Shya supplied.

"Yes, spontaneous. That's the word. It wasn't spontaneous."

"It actually became much easier to get distracted," Rod said. "Or to find an excuse not to have sex."

"So, what did you do to handle the birth control?" Ariel asked.

Rod and Caitlin glanced at each other, smiling with a trace of self-consciousness, while deciding how to answer. By unspoken agreement Rod once again took the lead. "We decided to use many different methods. We mixed it up. Caitlin got a diaphragm and we got condoms. We had some friends who had been monogamous for a while and they had decided to go on the pill so they had lots of extra condoms they no longer needed. They gave us a big bag," he said smiling.

"Condoms allow you to be spontaneous," Caitlin explained. "When you don't need to be spontaneous, then the diaphragm is good. It helped out a lot in terms of getting back to what we were used to. But we still haven't..." She glanced at us, not quite sure how to continue. It was obvious that the change in contraception had put a damper on their sex life. Physical intimacy had become more complicated and they hadn't yet regained their equilibrium.

"Well, here's my guess," Ariel offered. "If using a diaphragm is not spontaneous for you, then you haven't included using it as if it's as natural as taking off your bra, unzipping your pants or going to the bathroom. There's some way you're still looking at it like it's messy, it's gooey, it's odd. It's not a part of the natural flow of things."

"Yes!" Rod said.

"Yes," Caitlin confirmed, "that's totally true."

"Practice. Practice makes perfect," Shya suggested and they laughed, Caitlin rocking forward in her chair with delight.

"It took a lot of getting used to," she said with a smile. "But I'm better at it now. And, yeah, I haven't included it as a natural thing."

"Well, you know, it's okay to be an expert at it," Shya replied, "rather than it being something you put up with to get to the end result."

"Yes," Caitlin said, nodding, as she became thoughtful. It was as if she was replaying her approach to using a diaphragm in her mind and seeing it with fresh eyes and new possibilities.

"You see, it's not about getting to the end result. It's about where you are in each moment of the process called 'Your Life.' All of our lives are going to end at some point but what matters is where you are right now rather than trying to get it over with to get onto the better thing."

As Shya spoke you could see the wheels turning in both their minds. Rod let out a gentle laugh at his mental picture of the two of them wrestling with her diaphragm. For a moment he bent his head covering his face as he stifled a smile. "That is so true," he exclaimed.

"It makes it harder when you're trying to get it over with," Caitlin said.

"Absolutely, it makes it harder," Shya agreed. "We once knew a woman who was nursing her child and whenever she wanted it to be over with, her milk wouldn't flow and the kid would be fussy. When she finally surrendered to the fact that she was nursing, it was not problematic. The child stopped fussing, was calm and ate until he was sated. But when she was going somewhere, not simply being there with him, it was always difficult.

"When you're trying to get to the end result, it's always problematic because you're not where you are, and this is it. This is your life. This moment. Right now. This is it. All of it. Right now. This. Is. It."

Rod and Caitlin chuckled, calm yet excited at the same time.

"If you're not here in this moment, you're not here period," Shya continued. "No satisfaction, no well-being, because you're not there for it. It doesn't happen in the future because the future always comes down to a moment of now. If you're not here in your life, in each moment, then you have no satisfaction. And that includes putting in a diaphragm."

By now both Caitlin and Rod looked relaxed, no longer wincing at the mention of her diaphragm. The subject had ceased to be something messy or gooey or odd. It had become a natural thing much like unzipping your pants when no one is watching.

Now Ariel took the lead as if she were spinning a fairy tale, "Every girl has the dream of Prince Charming swooping in and putting all his attention on her…right up to the point where he might want to help you put your diaphragm in," she finished in a tongue-in-cheek manner. "You think, 'I want attention, I want wonderful, blissful sex. As long as you don't look at my body between my neck and my knees, we'll be fine.'"

Both Caitlin and Rod were laughing and nodding.

This described their situation to a tee.

"Yes," Caitlin laughed. "It is the embarrassment factor."

"Absolutely," Ariel said. "It's okay if you're having sex and his penis goes in your vagina because you're used to that, and that's where it fits as long as you don't have to look at it. Even if you love gazing at his naked body and he loves gazing at your naked body, it's different when you are specifically inserting your diaphragm. There is something very, very intimate and very personal about that."

Caitlin nodded, her brow furrowing, her nose wrinkling as she grimaced.

"And look at your face," Ariel laughed. "You're getting disgusted, as if that area is disgusting."

Caitlin laughed again. "I know!" she exclaimed.

"That is early programming," Shya explained. "You were bad for touching yourself down there."

"We were talking with somebody earlier today about people's prudish nature," Ariel said. "Life provides you with an opportunity to see what else is there. Everything was relaxed with birth control and now you have a different form of contraception and you get to see the little pockets of prudishness that you still have. It's kind of like cleaning your house and you find a drawer you had forgotten about that is full of junk."

"Mmm-hmm" they both said in unison, as they nodded in unison also. Caitlin and Rod were now back in sync.

"This is just your junk drawer. You're now cleaning it out. But I'm not saying your vagina is a junk drawer." Ariel grinned, wagging her finger at Caitlin in mock seriousness.

They both broke into gales of laughter. The difficulty of the subject had popped like a soap bubble.

"That's great," Caitlin said.

"Okay?" Ariel asked, by way of confirmation.

"Yeah! Absolutely! We'll have to include it in foreplay, because it's been like I go in the bathroom and shut the door," she laughed, "And 45 minutes later..."

"...I'm asleep." Rod laughed along with her.

"Don't be too long, please don't be very long," Shya sang, *"or I may be asleep."*

By now we had all gotten a bit silly—giddy at the thought of the ludicrousness of how they had been acting with each other. Our words fell over one another and laughter rang in the air.

"That's a great form of birth control!" Shya proclaimed with a laugh. "They never do it!'"

"Maybe you should get multiple diaphragms in all different colors and put them in different places all over the house," Ariel joked as she gestured, pretending to pluck one up. 'I'm in a purple mood dear,' or 'Let's go for the pink.' You could get a stars and stripes one when you're feeling patriotic."

"Oh, that's great!" Caitlin exclaimed.

"For the 4th of July," Rod said.

"Yes, then you could run it up the flagpole," Ariel said. We all laughed.

Caitlin and Rod had seen a new possibility and in that moment they were at ease with themselves and each other. You could tell that they were looking forward to "practicing" in the near future.

Birth Control and Intimacy
TransformationMadeEasy.com/matchmadeinheaven

37

ALCOHOL, SEX AND AGING

$\mathcal{A}$s the laughter died away and the diaphragm "issue" was resolved for the time being, Caitlin's next concerns about intimacy rose to the surface. She wondered if she could ask another question and we said, "Of course." Our conversation continued but now we were on to different subjects.

"I had the idea that as I got older I would want to have sex less," Caitlin stated. "But it's not true."

"How old are you?" Shya asked.

"41."

"Well, you have a lot of good years left as far as sex is concerned," Shya said.

"Yes, but I don't drink very much anymore," Caitlin said, "and we no longer go out the way we used to. Sex used to be very related to us going out."

"Going out and getting tipsy is just a device that you've used to lower your inhibitions," Ariel replied.

"Good point."

"Yes," Shya said, "you used alcohol to get you through those places where you have prudishness. It dulls that prudishness so you can get beyond it. But why not just experience the prudishness? If you allow yourself to feel your discomfort rather than mask it, it will dissolve away on its own. This is the Third Principle of Instantaneous Transformation."

"Yes," Caitlin said thoughtfully. Rod, too was nodding.

"There is a softer, wider, vaster," Ariel expanded her arms, "more powerful intimacy that comes when you don't have to use a device to drug you up in order to experience it."

"I'm just learning that," Caitlin admitted, "in conjunction with the diaphragm. It all came together at once. So everything became a lot more intimate really quickly."

"No, it didn't become more intimate. It became more confronting." Shya explained. "The intimacy is not in the confrontation. The intimacy is in letting go of the resistance to being seen. Because you think he is going to judge you the way you judge you. And the problem is, you are prejudiced against women, even though you are a woman."

"Yeah, I am," she said.

"Your prejudice is what's making you see yourself as disgusting. But God did not create anybody disgusting."

"Right." Caitlin turned to Rod who smiled back at her. "That's so true."

"Let's go back to the beginning of your question, Caitlin," Ariel said, "because you made such a powerful statement. You said that you had the idea that as you got older, sex had to slow down. And now that you're 41, you think that your sexual appetite has to diminish."

"We all have internalized ideas of how life should be at a certain age," Shya continued. "Milestone ideas. For example, we have unexamined beliefs about what happens when you get married, have a child or reach 65. We are socialized to think that at 65, you are retired and old and have lost your productivity or sense of purpose. There are many little milestones that have been slipped in, unconsciously for the most part. You've overheard people talking about their lives. 'Oh, when I hit 50 it was...' You internalized those statements and when you get close to that age, you suddenly think your life is over."

"I don't know why I did that,' Caitlin said, "but I did."

"Well," Shya said, "you probably heard somebody say it at one point."

"Go back a couple of generations in your family," Ariel suggested. "By the time somebody reached their 40s a few generations back, they would have wanted less sex. After all, they'd already had a dozen children and life expectancy a few hundred years ago was about 50. In those days, your family was consumed with having to stay alive, grow food and heat the house.

"Today, though, we don't have to grow our own food. In fact, it costs more for the two of us to grow food here in our back yard than it does to buy organic food from local farmers. You don't have to concern yourself with such things now, but, through the generations of your family, you absorbed that reality, unexamined. Now there is another possibility."

Rod and Caitlin looked at Ariel as she spoke, absorbing this new perspective.

"A little over a year ago," Ariel said, "I went to my doctor to tell her that I was concerned about feeling tired and draggy, that I didn't feel well. She said, 'Ariel, you are over 50 now, get used to it. Everyone over 50 is like that.' That was the last time I saw her. I found myself a new physician. My life is incredibly different now because I've had an active interest in possibility. You don't have to settle for a diminished life as you age."

"That is amazing," Caitlin said, her face alight.

"This stage in your life could be a new blossoming of possibility," Ariel said, "the possibility for you to be able to tolerate the regard of your partner."

"Yes," Caitlin turned to Rod again, "that's really true, right?"

He nodded and reached for her hand. She let her eyes fall to their fingers as they entwined. "I love that," Caitlin said. "Thank *you*."

"You're welcome," we said. "Thank you."

There are many myths about sexuality that we have all been socialized to believe. One of the most common is that people's sex drive diminishes significantly as they get older, especially if they've been married for many years. But we've been together for 30 years and this is not true for the two of us. Although we don't have sex with quite as much frequency as when we were in our 20s/40s (Ariel was 24 when we got together, Shya 41), we still enjoy having sex several times a week.

There are occasions when one of us is ill, or when we are extremely tired, where the frequency diminishes for a time. But we are always aware that if we go for too long without having physical intimacy we are off center, distracted by something. Sometimes we have been tempted to get lost in "getting ahead" in our career or sidetracked into various projects. Occasionally we have been surrounded by people who are fighting and whose relationships are in disarray and it has had an impact on the two of us. We frequently travel and sometimes we stay in an environment that isn't particularly conducive to romance. When this is the case, it's particularly important that we be attentive to taking care of ourselves and each other and not lose our sex drive. We have always had a passion for being with one another that includes physical intimacy. It's in the act of being with each other in this manner that we drop the cares of the day, find our center, and it still is a cornerstone for our Match Made in Heaven.

Alcohol, Sex and Aging
TransformationMadeEasy.com/matchmadeinheaven

38

LADIES AND GENTLEMEN,
START YOUR ENGINES

*H*ave you stopped to take a look at what starts your engine, what revs your sexual motor? Don't be shy. Take a look. If you know what supports your libido and what inhibits it, you can volitionally rev your sexual motor and get things restarted if things have gone a bit dry between you and your partner.

There may be particular scents or rituals that turn you on. For instance, if Shya shaves in the evening or Ariel asks him to shave, that is our clue that we plan to have sex before the night is through. Shya now makes his own shave oil with scents that we both find appealing. We tend to keep our bedroom clean so that things we have to do don't pull our eye or demand our attention when we are in the midst of making love.

Are you happier having sex in the morning or evening? Pay attention. Do you have certain activities that stoke your libido? One client of ours finds that when he volunteers at his kid's school by working on spreadsheets, he is always turned on when he returns home.

COLOR ME RED
One year, while browsing in a bookstore, Ariel decided to pick up a book in a genre that she had not read before.

Here is what happened in her own words:

It was a Thursday and I was in the local bookstore seeing how many copies of *Working on Yourself Doesn't Work* were on the shelves. Since I love to read, I decided to browse around to find a new book to bring home and relax with. I often gravitate toward fantasy fiction or detective novels. I like to call them "bubble gum books." These are books with "no nutritive value" but they are fun to consume.

On this day I was looking for something new when I happened upon the Romance section. I had never paid it much attention until this particular day when I found myself picking up an historical romance. I don't recall what the title was but I do remember that the cover was red. Within a few pages the heroine and hero began to have a torrid affair. I was surprised to see that this romance novel entailed scene after scene of a graphic sexual nature and that the writing was rather titillating. I bought the book.

That night, I read the first few chapters and I was happily surprised that it supported me in being even more desirous of Shya. The scenarios in that book revved up my engine and sex was all the more fun as a result. Shya was surprised and pleased as well. "What were you reading?" he asked. I showed him the cover.

I regularly read in the evenings before going to sleep. I find it relaxing and it's a good way for me to disengage from my day. But if I want to get a jump start on any sexual plans we may have for that night, Shya may find me reading a "red" book. And better still, he never has to worry about me reading a "regular" book until he is already asleep. I just say, "Don't worry. You won't make it through the night unmolested. Go ahead, fall asleep if you want. When I'm done with this book, I'll pick up a red one."

39

SEX, SEX, SEX, AND
DID WE MENTION... SEX?

*I*f you were raised in an environment where sex was considered bad or wrong or dirty, being self-expressive in a sexual way is foreign to you because you have inhibitions that were put in place at a very early age. It's almost as though there are invisible walls that you bounce up against without realizing it. When this happens, you think it's some flaw or fault in you, but it's nothing more than the conditioning of the culture in which you were raised.

Once again, our approach here is anthropological. It's about noticing the way you interact in your life and not judging yourself or blaming your parents or your upbringing for what you see.

Simply seeing it is enough to dissolve the constrictions around physical intimacy that dominate your life and your ability to relate with a partner.

BEING HERE
On our Internet radio show, *Being Here*, many episodes directly relate to creating and maintaining a magical relationship. We have addressed intimacy, personal respon-

sibility, the agenda to get married, listening, and looking for the prince or princess to come and save you. We have also done episodes on the topic of sex. As with our video mini-sessions, we are in awe of the honesty with which people express themselves when they call in with their questions. They are willing to reveal some of the most intimate details of their lives and their sex lives as well.

We had one such conversation with a young woman named Leah. She and her husband, Andy, have a fairly young marriage, since they wed earlier in the year. When Leah called, they were still learning about each other's bodies and expanding into their self-expression with one another in a physically intimate way. Unbeknownst to them, this sexual expansion lasts a lifetime if you let it. After three decades of being together, we are still learning new things about one another and experiencing a sweeter, deeper, richer and more intimate life with each other.

An astounding aspect of our conversation with Leah, along with her genuine interest in asking questions and listening to our answers, was the fact that her mother, Mary, was listening to the show. Ever since Leah and Andy introduced Mary to our books, seminars, videos and our radio show, transformation has become something special that they share as a family. It was sweet to see that she didn't ask questions in order to "shock" her mother, nor did she hold back. Join us as we have a frank conversation with Leah about a very personal topic: Sex with her husband.

SEX, SEX, SEX... AND
DID WE MENTION, SEX, TOO?

It was a crisp fall day when we started the second episode of our radio show on the topic of sex. The first show had been such a success, we asked our producer to promptly schedule a sequel. We had bought a popular magazine off the newsstands in preparation for the show as it had an article on how to bring heat to your sex life. We wanted to see what it had to offer.

On any given month, in *Cosmopolitan* or other such periodicals, you can find tips and rules, ideas and information about how to spice up or otherwise improve your sex life. But what we have discovered is that no matter what techniques you employ, it all comes back to "being here." If you are here for the experience of sexual intimacy, it can be a profound, heavenly event. But if you are lost in your thoughts, or trying to get somewhere (such as having an orgasm or not having an orgasm too soon), sex is but a shallow version of what is possible.

By now, we had already discussed the topics of listening and The Three Principles of Instantaneous Transformation. We had also chatted about the current issue of *Cosmo* and set the stage for our first caller that day. Here is the conversation:

"Hey, guys!" Leah began.

"Hi," we replied.

"Where are you calling in from today?" Ariel asked.

"I'm calling from New York," Leah said. "Oh my gosh," she continued, "you guys are so fun to listen to, I just enjoy you both so much and enjoy the radio show. I was nervous about calling in on a show that was about sex, but as I was just listening, I felt so much more relaxed. So thank you."

"Well, isn't it funny," Ariel said, "that we have sex compartmentalized as something to be embarrassed about? I mean if you were calling in on a show about your favorite food it would be far different."

"Yeah," Leah said with a laugh, "I probably wouldn't be so nervous."

"Yes, of course!" Ariel said. "You can say what your

favorite food is, but talking about your favorite things to do during sex would likely give you a different rush."

"Well, I do have a question for you," Leah said.

"Okay."

"Something has come up recently with my husband. We had this awesome sexy weekend where we just had fun and we had great sex and we felt really connected. And then just in the last couple of days, it's like—I don't know how to describe it—something shook things up. It's not like we've been fighting at all, but we haven't felt that kind of ease of intimacy and sex hasn't been effortless. It has felt more effortful, I guess. I just wonder, how do you get back on—like if you fall off the horse, how do you get back on the horse or husband, you know, where it's intimate and fun and easy?"

"Well, I'm left with a question," Shya said.

"Uh-hum."

"When did you speak to your mother last?"

"I think just yesterday." Leah replied.

"Yup," Ariel said, "And when did things get more bumpy?"

"I would say just in the last two days or so."

"Okay. So it may not be related, but sometimes people have a lack of flow around intimacy when in contact with family members," Ariel suggested.

"So your mother's coming to town," Shya said. "When is that?"

"In December for your course, The Freedom To Breathe and The Art of Being a Healer."

"Excellent, excellent," Shya said. Her answer had confirmed his suspicion.

"Yeah?" Leah asked. She wasn't yet tracking what he was seeing.

"Yeah," he said. "It's perfect that she's coming to town. You and your husband had great sex and it was very expressive and you were really there for it. Could you tell your mother about it?"

"Ummm..." Leah said clearly uncomfortable.

"Yeah, maybe now you can because she listens to this show," Ariel said.

"Yeah," Leah said laughing, "Hi, Mom! I mean she knows that we do have great sex. But we don't talk about it, no. Not the specifics of it."

"It's not that I'm making your mother the problem here at all," said Shya. "It's just that you've been programmed to not be sexual."

"Yes, that's true."

"When you were three or four years old, you touched yourself and people slapped your hand," Shya said.

"Right," Leah replied.

"But it felt good to touch yourself," Shya said. "You know you have a lot of nerve plexus in that area that feels good, but playing with yourself was not acceptable. We have some friends who have two sons and the younger one keeps dropping down on his belly and basically humping the floor. The older boy says, "Mom, he keeps rubbing the floor!" But the mother knows that this youngster is doing that because it feels good, it excites him and that it's something he's likely to grow out of. Since it's something he only does at home, since he's not dropping down in the supermarket or at school, she's being patient with it."

"Most of us didn't grow up in that type of a household," Ariel said.

"True," Shya agreed. "Most of us didn't have a liberal parent who was willing to allow us to feel what we were feeling when we began to explore our sexuality."

"Right," Leah said.

"Sometimes, Leah," Ariel added, "when you've spoken to somebody or you're getting ready to speak to somebody like your mom, you kind of reel things back in so as to be proper by the time you get to the phone call.

"But Shya and I used to really go through what you are describing. When we would have that sexual expansion, it was often challenging afterwards for a period of time because some part of us wanted to get things back in control, to get it back to the normal scope of things. But we didn't just get 'back to normal.' We contracted. It's as if we automatically zigzagged back to being more closed up."

"Yeah, that's how it's felt this last week," Leah said. "Like it was really, really playful and fun and then it zigzagged back."

"What else has happened in the last week?" Shya asked.

"It really resonated when you were talking earlier in the show about how you act in your life you will carry over to your sex life. Like if you're ahead of yourself in your daily life, when you approach your partner in a sexual or intimate way, you'll be ahead of yourself or you won't be able to really be there. I've noticed it when I jump out ahead of myself in projects at work and in other areas as well."

"Right," Shya said. "If you're trying to get somewhere all the time, then you bring that to your intimate time. Then you're not really there. You're waiting to get somewhere that's going to be better than where you are and you never get there."

"Yeah," Leah said.

"You said it was playful about a week ago," Ariel said. "But last week has already devolved into a concept. At this point it is no longer an experience, but rather just a trace memory of how it used to be."

"Comparing this moment to that moment is a killer. Comparison absolutely kills," Shya said.

"Oh, yeah," Leah said. She could easily see how she

had been doing this.

"If you compare the sex you're having today with the sex you had on a previous day and think that was better, you won't actually be there with your husband. People often hold onto the good memories for comparisons, but they're only memories. They're not actually an experience any longer," Shya said.

"Right, yeah," Leah replied.

"You know, Leah," Ariel said, "Shya and I have been together 30 years and trust me in that time, we've had lots of orgasms."

"Really, really, really, lots and lots and lots!" Shya said playfully.

"Awesome," Leah said.

"Some of them were explosive," Ariel said. "And some of them were what I would term 'squeaky.' You know, you have an orgasm but there isn't a lot of sensation and you kind of say to yourself, 'What? That was all? That's not fair.' Whether it's caused by rushing things, being overtired to begin with, not quite being in my body or my hormones being slightly out of whack, it happens from time to time."

"But if you worry about having a 'squeaky' orgasm, for instance," Shya said, "you force it to happen over and over again. If there's something you're resisting, you keep it around."

"Yes, I see that," Leah said.

Ariel smiled to herself and said, "This reminds me of a grade school off-color joke, Leah. It's about a guy who goes to a house of ill repute where there are three floors of ladies to service the men. On the ground floor there is a gorgeous, gorgeous woman. There is a middle-aged lady on the middle floor, and upstairs there is a well-seasoned lady who used to be a school teacher. Even though she is by far the oldest and the most expensive of all three, there's a huge line outside her door. At the end of the joke the man finally says, "Well, I'll try the one on the top floor, as it seems like she's really popular." He climbs to the third floor to take his place in line when he hears her say to her current client, "If I've told you once, I've told you a thousand times, practice, practice, practice. Okay, now, let's do it again until you get it right!"

Leah laughed as she got the punch line.

"If you're not feeling like you're having fun, practice, practice, practice!" Ariel said.

"But then," Shya added, "the opposite is true. If you are feeling you're having fun, practice, practice, practice!"

"Practice, right. I'll do that," Leah said, with amusement. "Awesome. I like that. Can I ask one more quick question?"

"Sure," Shya said.

"It doesn't even have to be quick." Ariel added.

"Okay," Leah said, taking a more serious tone. "I'm a little embarrassed but it's about blowjobs."

"Okay," Ariel said.

"Basically since I've been with my husband, it's like a whole new world has opened up and I've enjoyed giving him a blowjob in a way that I never have before. And it's been fun. But I have this thing about swallowing."

"Swallowing cum?" Shya asked.

"Yes."

"Uh-hum," Shya said by way of encouragement.

"I always chicken out at the last minute. I have this idea that it's uncomfortable or gross or whatever," Leah said a bit haltingly.

"First of all, where did you get the idea that to swallow is better or not to swallow is better?" Ariel said.

"I definitely have the idea that to swallow is better," Leah said.

"Okay. Where did you get that idea?" Shya asked.

"Gosh, I must have had it since I was a teenager or something." It was obvious that Leah was actually looking at the question for the first time. She had never before stopped to look at the pressure she put on herself to swallow her husband's semen when they were having oral sex.

"You know what, it might have even been my high school boyfriend," she said with a laugh. "I'm having a vague memory of this and it probably goes back to adolescence somewhere."

"Here's something I've learned about myself over the years." Ariel said "If there's something about sex that I repeatedly think about, it's generally something that I want. If what you've been thinking about is being able to comfortably swallow semen, chances are it's something you have an interest in."

"Uh-hum," Leah said.

"You may get your husband to request it," Shya said. "You are totally capable of manipulating him into caring one way or the other, whether you swallow or not."

"Right, right," Leah said.

"But, you know," Ariel continued, "you could think about it like Nike and 'Just do it!' It's not a whole lot different than saliva—just thicker."

Leah laughed as the subject had taken on a lightness and ease.

"Or you can think of it like Jell-O shooters," Ariel said with a smile in her voice. "We hear that's a popular drink. You can trick yourself any way you want. But it's interesting—the whole disgust factor that you've been trained with."

"We've been enculturated into thinking that sex is a disgusting thing but between you and your husband, it shouldn't be," Shya said.

"When you're really hot, things get juicy and gooey and messy and you know what, that's part of the fun of sex," Ariel said.

"Uh-hum. Yeah. Cool!" Leah said.

"By the way," Ariel said, "if you're backing off from some aspect of something that you want during sex, that tends to make sex less playful."

"You may have just come up with your own answer, Leah," Shya said.

"Cool. That's awesome. Thanks so much guys."

"Thanks for calling in," Shya said.

"Thanks for being so honest and forthcoming," Ariel added.

"You guys have a great day."

"Okay. And Leah?" Ariel said before moving on to the next caller.

"Yes?"

"Don't forget: Practice, practice, practice!"

"Of course! Thanks. I can hardly wait."

Sex, Sex, Sex...and Did We Mention Sex, too?
TransformationMadeEasy.com/matchmadeinheaven

40

PRACTICE, PRACTICE, PRACTICE

*N*ow that you have read this book, we expect it has been an organic, living, breathing journey for you, similar to a relationship. Take a moment now and look back at the Table of Contents or flip back through the book and randomly pick pages to read. You will likely find certain ideas that seemed foreign at first have now been seamlessly integrated into your reality. All that's left is for you to practice: Practice being in the moment and practice being you. This will not be not be difficult to do since you are already in the moment, this moment of your life, and you are a *perfect you*.

Now that we have taken this journey together, you have discovered the good news: You can't be different than you are in the current moment of your life. In other words, your current life circumstances can only be exactly as they are. You have also seen that anything you resist follows you through life and if you allow your life to be as it is, your problems complete themselves. That takes the pressure off. All you have to do is notice how you are being in the current moment of your life without judging yourself or blaming others or the circumstances for what you see. This is enough to transform both your life and your ability to relate.

What it takes is slowing down—just a little bit—enough to access the current moment of your life. This is not a one-time thing. This is part of a transformational lifestyle. We have all been programmed and conditioned to get somewhere in the future, to achieve or to produce some result. But what we are presenting here is a new possibility to be with the events of your life in each moment rather than trying to fulfill some childhood dream or decision.

Throughout this book, we have met courageous individuals who have sat down with us to ask questions. And they have been kind enough to share their stories, foibles and greatness with you. Since each individual presented a facet of the gem called "relationship," it's easy to see oneself in them. Their humanity and magnificence has been a true inspiration. If you slow down—just a little bit—you may touch on your own humanity and magnificence as well.

This journey now ends where we began. In the early pages we stated:

If after reading this book, you only had one benefit—being kind to yourself—we would consider it an overwhelming success. This is because:

Heaven on Earth begins with You.

INDEX

ACKNOWLEDGEMENTS

First and foremost we wish to thank again those individuals who are highlighted in the videos and radio shows. Without you, your honesty, courage and willingness to be seen, there would be no book. We are grateful to our friend Menna de sa Baretto (A.K.A. Menna Van Praag) for her talented assistance throughout this project. You are *simply brilliant!* Special thanks to Rod Hill for his wonderful videography and video editing. Our editor Andrea Cagan was, once again, a dream come true. We really enjoy being "Caganized." Thanks to Frances Rutherford for making sure that we crossed our 't's and dotted our 'i's and to Arne Hoffmann for our cover photo. Fernanda Franco – your design work rocks and Susan Donlon we are blessed to have you as the producer of *Being Here*. We are also grateful to our behind the scenes, exceptional support staff, Valerie Paik and Christina Sayler for your professionalism and friendship. We appreciate you every day more than you know. Also, thanks again to our amazing website company TAG Online, who got us up on the web before we even knew what it was. The videos that are the backbone of this book have been presented with your genius and technical wizardry.

ABOUT THE KANES

Since 1987, award-winning authors Ariel and Shya Kane have taught individuals, couples and organizations across the globe how to live in the moment. Acting as Catalysts for Instantaneous Transformation, they inspire people to unwire the knee-jerk behaviors that get in the way of living life with ease. The Kanes' approach has a unique flavor that is designed for modern-day circumstances and complexities while resonating with the universal truths of the ages.

Together for 30 years and counting, people still ask Ariel and Shya if they are on their honeymoon. Their acclaimed best-seller *How to Create a Magical Relationship* was the gold medal winner of the 2007 Nautilus Book Award in the category of Relationships / Men & Women's Issues.

To access their radio show, event schedule, join the Premium Excellence Club, or to find out more, visit: www.TransformationMadeEasy.com.

 Bonus Video – Transformation on the River
TransformationMadeEasy.com/matchmadeinheaven